Essays on International Asset Management:
Evidence for Developed West and Emerging East

STUDIEN ZU INTERNATIONALEN WIRTSCHAFTSBEZIEHUNGEN

Herausgegeben von Prof. Dr. Michael Frenkel

Band 17

PETER LANG
Frankfurt am Main · Berlin · Bern · Bruxelles · New York · Oxford · Wien

Marina Nikiforow

Essays on International Asset Management: Evidence for Developed West and Emerging East

PETER LANG
Internationaler Verlag der Wissenschaften

Bibliographic Information published by the Deutsche Nationalbibliothek
The Deutsche Nationalbibliothek lists this publication in the Deutsche Nationalbibliografie; detailed bibliographic data is available in the internet at http://dnb.d-nb.de.

Zugl.: Hannover, Univ., Diss., 2010

D 89
ISSN 1618-503X
ISBN 978-3-631-61794-6

www.peterlang.de

Table of contents

1. Introduction

1.1 Motivation and contribution of this dissertation

Asset management is a global business which has spread from developed financial centers to emerging and transition[1] markets. Investment professionals manage huge volumes of assets and thus possess potential to influence not only asset pricing, but also economic development – obviously demonstrated by the recent financial crisis. Hence, knowledge about the investment behavior of this important group of investors is valuable as it helps to elucidate price movements on international financial markets.

The relevance of professional asset managers can be best highlighted by the role assigned to them in the finance theory. To explain financial markets, the traditional finance framework provides models with "rational" agents and "informational efficient" markets: Investors are assumed to process all available information and thus correctly form their expectations about securities' future cash flows. In that case, a security's actual price reflects its true "fundamental value" – the discounted sum of expected future cash flows. This prominent Efficient Market Hypothesis (EMH), differentiating the weak-, semistrong- and strong-form market efficiency, has been formulated by Fama (1970). Moreover, in efficient markets there are no unexploited profit opportunities ("no free lunch"). The early work by Friedman (1953) suggests that even if not all investors were fully rational, the group of rational investors would quickly eliminate any deviation from a security's fundamental value, i.e. a mispricing, caused by irrational traders. Rational traders are thus considered as "arbitrageurs" or "smart money", who make riskless profits at no cost by exploiting mispricing and thus pushing prices back towards their fundamental values.

However, raising prominent questions such as "Do stock prices move too much to be justified by subsequent changes in dividends?" by Shiller (1981) and "Does the stock market overreact?" by De Bondt und Thaler (1985) have challenged the EMH in the early 1980. "Excess volatility", "market overreaction", and "mean reversion" have been empirically disclosed. These so-called market anomalies, i.e. price developments, which are not in line with the EMH, question the rationality and riskless arbitrage opportunities in the markets. Moreover, these findings initiated the Behavioral Finance as a new finance approach to better understand financial markets. Behavioral finance mainly

1 Transition markets are those economies transforming from a central planning system to a market system. They can be regarded as a subgroup of emerging markets.

builds on two concepts, both relaxing the assumption of the EMH (Barberis and Thaler, 2003). First, theoretical models (e.g. Shleifer and Summers, 1990) show that there are "limits to arbitrage" in markets due to fundamental risks and unpredictability of future resale prices, which retain arbitrageurs from fully eliminating mispricing. Thus, irrational traders, also referred to as "noise traders" or "liquidity traders", can cause substantial and long-lived price deviations from fundamental values. Second, behavioral finance incorporates "investor psychology" by relying on insights from extensive experimental evidence provided by cognitive psychologists: Prominent work by e.g. Kahneman and Tversky (1974) detects "heuristics and biases" in people's "judgment under uncertainty", implying that people are not fully rational, but subject to systematic biases when forming their beliefs.

In sum, one core goal of behavioral finance is it to show that some financial market phenomena can be better understood by using models in which some agents are *not fully* rational. For example, behavioral finance models aim to explain the phenomenon of the profitability of momentum strategies (buying winning stocks and selling losing stocks) documented in Jegadeesh and Titman (1993) by investors' overreaction to new information. Such biased information processing is attributable to investors' cognitive biases, i.e. conservatism bias and representative heuristic as well as self-attribution bias and overconfidence (Barberis et al., 1998, Daniel et al., 1998, Hong and Stein, 1999). Thus, the psychologically motivated overreaction to new information can push prices away from their fundamental values and lead to formation of price trends, which would enable momentum profits. Indeed, Jegadeesh and Titman (2001) find supportive evidence for the overreaction hypothesis.

In the real world, professional asset managers are the typical arbitrageurs. Compared to private investors, they possess comparative advantages regarding professional education, information availability, and investment volume. However, studies have documented that also this group of sophisticated investors is subject to behavioral biases (for an overview see Hirshleifer, 2001, Barberis and Thaler, 2003). Moreover, professionalism may reduce some biases, but fails to eliminate them entirely (e.g. Feng and Seasholes, 2005, Shapira and Venezia, 2006).

Against this background, the need for detailed empirical analyses of asset managers' investment processes is justified by their central role in the traditional finance theory with respect to market efficiency and additionally strengthened by the behavioral finance evidence on biases in their investment behavior. How persistent are professional investors' biases? Can training on behavioral finance help to better recognize and avoid psychological traps within their own investment process? Furthermore, even though basic investment theories are the same worldwide, market environments in developed, emerging, and transition markets differ in their institutional and regulatory settings as well as market transparency. In turn, different investment environments are likely to leave their mark on fund managers' investment practices. Are there any specifics in the information processing and investment behavior of fund managers from developed, emerging, and transition markets? Such knowledge would help investors to better understand the movement of securities prices in the respective market environments. In addition, of particular interest is whether fund managers' investment behavior contributes to market efficiency in less developed and less transparent markets.

This dissertation aims to clarify these questions. An international academic survey project with asset managers from the developed West and the emerging East provides relevant data on these important market players' views, perceptions and investment behavior.[2] This questionnaire survey was conducted in the Western developed markets USA and Germany (117 participants in Germany in 2002; 412 participants in both markets in 2003/04), the Asian emerging market Thailand (126 participants in 2004), as well as in the Eastern European transition markets Russia and Ukraine (116 participants in 2007/08). Such a broad international sample allows not only for country-specific analyses, but also for even more interesting cross-country comparisons. Overall, we report a firm participation rate of 48% and 772 worldwide received questionnaires from 274 investment companies.[3]

The survey questionnaire contains statements, tasks and questions, which have been formulated based on theoretical behavioral finance hypotheses as well as former empirical findings on investors' behavior. In detail, we are interested in fund managers' perception of prominent behavioral biases in the market, self-perception regarding own investment biases, risk attitudes, incentives, the use of various information sources and investment strategies, investment allocation preferences as well as their personal characteristics. Before starting the survey, several interviews were held with fund managers in the financial centers of the USA and Germany, as well as in Bangkok, Moscow, and Kiev. These pre-survey interviews served to ensure that questionnaire contents and response

---

2 I highly appreciate the possibility to also use the data which has been collected by my colleagues Torben Lütje and Daniela Beckmann within our international academic research project on "Behavioral patterns and their determinants in the investment process of institutional investors".

3 Former survey studies on institutional investors by e.g. Shiller and Pound (1989) and Bodnar et al. (1996) report response rates of 45% and 18%, respectively.

categories are formulated in an appropriate and accepted manner.[4] For enabling reliable cross-country comparisons, the wording in the respective survey languages, i.e. English, German and Russian, has been assured to be correct, well understood and express the same issue. Moreover, guaranteed anonymity to all participants as well as the offer to provide them with survey results gives low incentives for strategic answering.[5]

The key to the survey success were relevant recommendation letters and organizational support provided by national investment management associations in Germany, Thailand, Russia, and Ukraine. We therefore thank the German Investment Association "BVI", the Thai Association of Investment Management Companies "AIMC", the Russian National League of Asset Managers "NLU", and the Ukrainian Association of Investment Business "UAIB". Furthermore, our whole survey project team highly appreciates the constructive comments by our pre-survey interview partners and thanks all participating asset managers for their interest in the project and time spent to respond to our questionnaire.

1.2 Outline

The remainder of this dissertation proceeds as follows: Chapter 2 and 3 focus on the German asset management industry. They shed light on the persistence of fund managers' behavioral biases. Expanding to comparative cross-country analyses, Chapters 4 and 5 examine the influence of different market settings (in developed, emerging and transition markets) on two major elements of fund managers' investment process – their information processing and investment behavior. One special contribution of this dissertation is the evidence provided for fund managers in Eastern European transition markets. Though Eastern Europe has become an attractive investment region in the past decade, academic research on its financial markets is still scarce. Thus, Chapter 6 aims to further extend evidence on so far rarely addressed Eastern European transition markets and provides another relevant analysis for international asset management: The study of the exchange rate exposure of Eastern European exporting firms.

4 The questionnaire as well as indications for country-specific adaptations are included in the Annex.

5 Bonus payments are generally considered as a confidential compensation detail. However, over 70% of our surveyed fund managers have indicated the size of their bonus (relative to their base salary). This fact certainly confirms their trust in an anonymous and confidential treatment of their answers (which we pointed out in each questionnaire) and thus their open-minded attitude towards the whole survey.

Chapter 2 questions whether professionals' *endorsement of behavioral finance* has any influence on their perception of markets and themselves. Particularly, this chapter provides evidence on the hypothesis that many behavioral finance patterns are so deeply rooted in human behavior that they are difficult to overcome by learning. We test this on a target group which has undoubtedly very strong incentives to learn efficient behavior, i.e. fund managers. We split this group into endorsers and non-endorsers of behavioral finance. Endorsers do, indeed, view markets differently as they perceive stronger influences from behavioral biases. However, when it comes to the perception of one's own behavior the endorsement of behavioral finance becomes almost meaningless, even though endorsers otherwise do adapt behavior towards their conviction. The results of our study demonstrate the persistence of behavioral patterns even with knowledge of their existence and thus their dominance over rational learning. The challenge for professional fund managers, in particular for those with insight in behavioral finance, consists therefore in a more critical assessment of own investment behavior in order to discipline and rationalize it.

Chapter 3 deepens the previous analysis by addressing the concern that failure to recognize own biases will prevent from striving to correct them. This chapter therefore provides survey evidence on the influence of *training* on behavioral finance on professional fund managers' perception and investment behavior. In particular, it examines whether "trained" fund managers differ from the "untrained" ones in their perception of markets and themselves as well as in their choice of information sources and investment strategies. Additionally, the influence of integration of behavioral finance approaches into investment processes is also considered. The results reveal that training on behavioral finance basically intensifies the perception of biases in the behavior of others – especially the reflection effect and the home bias. Training also reduces the affinity to conformity, leading to less reliance on colleagues and other market participants as information sources. However, pure training is insufficient to significantly affect fund managers' investment behavior, but behavioral finance approaches need to be integrated into investment processes.

Changing to international cross-country analyses, **Chapter 4** examines fund managers' *information processing*, being the basis for intelligent decision-making. In particular, it provides supportive survey evidence for the hypothesis that fund managers' information processing differs between Western developed markets (DM) and Eastern European transition markets (TM) – two market settings rich in institutional differences. We unveil two core findings: Compared to fund managers in the USA and Germany (DM), their peers in Russia and Ukraine (TM) stand out due to higher relevance assigned to order flows and a higher level of herding. Investigating whether these TM-features may represent price discovery mechanisms in less transparent TM, we find evidence in favor of price discovery in the positive relation between the orientation on fundamental information and herd behavior in TM, most obviously in Ukraine. In contrast, in both DM and TM, order flow analysis lacks fundamental orientation, thus indicating it to contain rather short-lived semi-fundamental information. Furthermore, the influence of company size on fund managers' information processing differs between DM and TM. In DM, rather smaller companies tend to both, observing order flows and following trends (herding). Interestingly, in TM, these are smaller companies who follow trends, but bigger ones who are more interested in order flow – probably due to their privileged access to it. This would further confirm order flow to contain rather short-lived semi-fundamental information.

Chapter 5 extends the previous analysis by addressing another element of fund managers' investment process, i.e. their *investment behavior*. This chapter presents survey evidence on the hypothesis that asset managers from emerging markets behave more biased than do their peers from developed markets. This hypothesis arises from the assumption that an emerging market's environment might induce more biased investment actions due to e.g. its lower market transparency and information efficiency or its scarce professional training opportunities. The above hypothesis is tested by comparing our emerging market sample from Russia and Thailand with the developed one from Germany as reference market. Thereby, we focus on asset managers' risk behavior, which is crucial for investment decision-making, as well as on their propensity to two highly discussed behavioral puzzles, i.e. herding and home bias. Indeed, compared to their German peers, we find asset managers from emerging markets to declare a more biased behavior, i.e. regarding loss aversion and disposition effect as well as herding and home bias. Furthermore, we identify both latter biases to be significantly influenced by the former two. For the home-biased asset allocation in the two emerging markets, strong regulatory influence and fund managers' personal characteristics are found to matter in addition.

Overall, the evidence in Chapters 4-5 suggests that the quality of an investment environment significantly affects fund managers' investment process, including information processing and investment behavior.

Deepening the focus on (so far rarely addressed) *Eastern Europe*, **Chapter 6** analyzes the *exchange rate exposure* of exporting firms in Eastern European transition economies, i.e. Russia and the three EU accession countries Czech Republic, Poland, Hungary (CEEC-3). This study also controls for possible effects of different exchange rate regimes. For over 80% of our sample, we find fluctuations in the US Dollar and Euro rates to have a significant impact on firms' stock returns. However, the magnitude and direction of firms' exposure depends on the particular exchange rate and clearly differs between Russia and the CEEC-3. We find that the exposure is only to the US Dollar and negative in Russia, but mostly to the Euro and positive in the CEEC-3.[6] These results are even stronger at the firm level. Such substantial differences may result from a differing dominance of exposure channels in the respective economies, such as the country-specific export structure and foreign debt. Finally, the switch from a fixed to a flexible exchange rate regime appears to be less important for the exchange rate exposure. The results of this study are of interest for both, investors and researchers. For investors, since the reference currency as well as country-specific structures matter for the direction and strength of exchange rate exposure; for researchers, since pooling firms from various countries may weaken the results.

All in all, this dissertation aims to enrich insights on international asset management, particularly on the influential investment behavior of fund managers around the world, i.e. in the USA, Germany, Russia, Ukraine, and Thailand. The presented survey evidence does not only confirm prior empirical findings, but also provides new valuable results: The investment behavior of professional fund managers is not fully determined by rational reactions to fundamental information. In fact, also fund managers' viewpoints and perception, particularly their attitude towards behavioral finance as well as their home market's institutional environment leave their mark on fund managers' information processing and investment behavior. Furthermore, the extent to which fund managers are subject to biases seem to increase in less developed markets. These findings should help sharpen investment professionals' awareness of the persistence of behavioral biases that might affect their investment performance. Global investors should take into account that there are differences in investment processes in the developed West and the emerging East. I hope this dissertation contributes to improve the understanding of the financial world from both, the academic as well as the practical perspective.

6 Negative (positive) exposure means that a depreciation of the domestic currency goes along with an increase (decrease) of share prices.

2. Professionals' endorsement of behavioral finance: Does it impact their perception of markets and themselves?[7]

2.1 Introduction

The history of many anomalies in financial markets has shown that they disappear over time (Fama, 1998). This has raised the suspicion that markets may need time to recognize such anomalies – which largely motivate behavioral finance – but that they react consequently afterwards. According to this view one may assess behavioral finance being largely concerned with transitory phenomena. Others argue that many behavioral finance patterns are so deeply rooted in human behavior that they are difficult to overcome by learning (Alpert and Raiffa, 1982, Fischhoff, 1982b, Tversky and Kahneman, 1982, and more recently Hirshleifer, 2001). Obviously, these two views make contrary predictions on the persistence of behavioral phenomena although both camps agree that in the long run fundamentals drive prices. If rational learning is dominant then one could expect that insights into behavioral finance impact one's own behavior. If, however, learning mechanisms are weak in this respect the insights into behavioral finance will have a minor impact on one's own behavior. We provide a test of these competing views and find evidence in support of the latter hypothesis put forward by psychologists working in behavioral decision-making and more recently by behavioral economists.[8]

Our research aims for extending literature in psychology which has clearly revealed the "bias blind spot" (Pronin et al., 2002), i.e. the belief that one's own

---

7 I would like to thank my co-author Lukas Menkhoff. This paper was originally published in Journal of Economic Behavior & Organization 71:2, 2009, 318-329, under the title "Professionals' endorsement of behavioral finance: Does it impact their perception of markets and themselves?", and is reproduced by kind permission of Elsevier. We thank all participating fund managers for their time and commitment; we thank participants at the German Economic Association Conference in Munich and at the European Financial Management Association Conference in Athens for their useful discussion. Moreover, we gratefully acknowledge the useful comments of two anonymous referees and research assistance by Torsten Brozynski.

8 Nowadays it is widely accepted that behavioral finance builds on two concepts, i.e. "investor psychology" and "limits to arbitrage" (see Shleifer and Summers, 1990; Barberis and Thaler, 2002).

judgments are less susceptible to biases than the judgments of others.[9] We extend this research by addressing an important objection that economists might voice against evidence based on student surveys: The probability that behavioral biases hold depends on how strong incentives are to learn and thus to overcome entrenched behavior. One can easily imagine circumstances where people adhere to behavioral patterns as forecast by behavioral finance just because their welfare is not at stake. It seems therefore advisable for an empirical examination of the hypothesis put forward by psychologists and behavioral economists to choose a target group that has undoubtedly strong incentives to learn. We have thus targeted professional fund managers. Their investment performance is on the one hand negatively affected by behavioral biases (see e.g. Shefrin and Statman, 1985, Coval and Shumway, 2005, Biais and Weber, 2007) and on the other permanently monitored and linked to high performance-related bonuses. Among these fund managers we differentiate between "endorsers" of behavioral finance and others, who we call "non-endorsers".

Endorsers of behavioral finance are those fund managers who believe that the approach of behavioral finance truly reflects decision behavior in fund management (and who know the key messages of behavioral finance well). In contrast to them are non-endorsers, i.e. fund managers who are not that much convinced about the relevance of behavioral finance. We have surveyed more than 100 fund managers in Germany and classify them according to their self-assessment into these two groups. We then analyze whether fund managers' endorsement of behavioral finance, i.e. being an "endorser", impacts their perception of markets and themselves: do these groups respond in the same way to questionnaire items addressing, first, their perception of general fund managers' behavior and, second, their perception of their own behavior with respect to issues being raised by behavioral finance research?

We find a revealing split in responses: whereas endorsers recognize significantly stronger behavioral finance effects in other fund managers' behavior than non-endorsers, the perception of their own behavior is largely unaffected by their insights. When endorsers are asked about their own behavior with respect to items being linked to behavioral finance, such as hindsight bias or disposition effect, they answer as non-endorsers do. However, there is one exception to this pattern: endorsers show less miscalibration with respect to forecasting the interval of a stock index. As less miscalibration here also means

9 This asymmetry arises from the stance of "naive realism" as well as from different strategies people apply to detect bias in own judgments versus the judgments of others (Pronin et al., 2004; see also Ehrlinger et al., 2005). Recent research in this line includes adding individual's self-image to the utility function (Johansson-Stenman and Martinsson, 2006).

more correct answers, this suggests that endorsers' conviction of behavioral finance may increase awareness for respective distortions and can improve decisions to some extent.

In a final exercise, we analyze whether endorsers' assessment of their own behavior may reflect the fact that behavioral finance does not influence their decisions in any respect. Therefore, we ask whether endorsers differ from non-endorsers regarding two further items of investment behavior, i.e. their preferred information sources and investment strategies. We find that both groups seem to differ clearly in their use of information sources although not to a statistically significant extent. The difference becomes significant, however, with respect to preferred investment strategies as endorsers rely more on momentum and contrarian strategies. We conclude that endorsers do not generally behave like non-endorsers, making the above found indifference between both groups with respect to their self-assessment more credible.

Thus, we come back to the hypothesis – proposed by psychologists and behavioral economists – that many behavioral patterns are difficult to overcome by learning. Our findings provide support for his view as insight into behavioral finance and thus into the behavior of others does not easily change one's own behavior. We regard it as an important and innovative aspect of our research that this result has been found among fund managers because this target group has strong incentives to improve behavior. In this respect we also find a partial justification for Fama's (1998) optimism into learning processes in that the endorsement of behavioral finance reduces miscalibration.

The remaining study is structured into four sections. Section 2.2 describes data of the questionnaire survey. The following sections present our analyses, starting with views on the market's behavior (Section 2.3), then views on one's own behavior (Section 2.4) and, finally, consequences on investment behavior (Section 2.5). Section 2.6 concludes.

2.2 Data

This study is based on a questionnaire survey that addressed all relevant fund management companies in Germany between 15 August and 12 December, 2002 and yielded a useful and largely representative sample.

Table 2.1: Descriptive statistics of respondents

Item asked	*Responses (in per cent)*			Number of responses
Age (in years)	<35: *50.9*	35-45: *46.5*	>45: *2.6*	114
Professional experience (in years)	<5: *22.3*	5-15: *59.8*	>15: *17.9*	112
Gender	Male: *92.1*	Female: *7.9*		114
Share of bonus payment	Mean: *25.8*	Std. dev.: *14.5*		85
University degree	Yes: *84.8*	No: *15.2*		112
Governing position	Yes: *36.9*	No: *63.1*		103
Kind of fund management (primarily)	Active: *93.7*	Passive: *6.3*		111
Kind of securities managed [(a)]	Stocks: *66.5*	Bonds: *33.5*		115

(a) 4.2% of the respondents managed stocks and bonds to the same degree. These respondents were added with half weight to stocks as well as bonds, so that the sum adds up to 100%.

In total, out of the 59 relevant fund management companies 35 participated in the survey, with at least one appropriate questionnaire each. This resulted in a response rate of 59 percent concerning participated fund management companies.[10]

To ensure the reliability of responses many intensive interviews with fund managers were conducted in advance of the survey. These interviews served to formulate questions in an appropriate manner. Furthermore, in later stages the questionnaire was used in a pre-test with several fund managers as a final check of its acceptance and appropriateness. Feedback indicates that the response is useful for our research purpose.

The descriptive statistics in *Table 2.1* provide a picture of personal characteristics of the respondents in this survey. Accordingly, the mean of responding fund managers shows an age of about 35 years, has professional experience of 10 years, is of male gender, earns a bonus payment of 25 percent, has a university degree, works rather in a non-governing position, practices active fund management and manages stocks rather than bonds. This data is consistent with the information from similar surveys in Germany such as Menkhoff (1998) or Arnswald (2001).

10 The structure of this response is largely similar to the industry's structure. Our sample is representative in this sense (see Appendix 1).

Table 2.2: Endorsers and non-endorsers

[BF1] Statement: "The research findings in behavioral finance reflect decision behavior in fund management".

[BF2] Statement: "I've already concerned myself with behavioral finance, the key messages are well known to me".

Distribution of responses (frequencies)								
		BF1: Research findings reflect decision behavior in fund management (complete approval – complete contradiction)						
		1	**2**	**3**	**4**	**5**	**6**	Σ
BF2: Key messages of behavioral finance are well known to respondent	**1**	5	20	7	2	0	-	*34*
	2	1	11	17	4	2	-	*35*
	3	0	2	9	5	5	-	*21*
	4	0	1	4	5	4	-	*14*
	5	0	0	2	0	1	-	*3*
	6	-	-	-	-	-	-	-
	Σ	*6*	*34*	*39*	*16*	*12*	-	***107***

As basis for the formation of groups our questionnaire contains two useful statements on behavioral finance, i.e. endorsement and knowledge of behavioral finance. These statements are given in *Table 2.2* as BF1 and BF2, both of which are assessed by 6 answering categories, ranging from "complete approval" (coded as 1) to "complete contradiction" (coded as 6). The main information we use from these statements is the degree of endorsement of behavioral finance as it is expressed in the response to BF1. Due to the distribution of answers (see the contingency table in Table 2.2) we define endorsers by comprising answering categories 1 and 2, whereas category 3 seems to characterize an intermediate stance in comparison to the sample. We complement this definition by information from BF2, i.e. we define that endorsers should also know the key messages of behavioral finance well (corresponding to answering categories 1 and 2 again).[11]

11 Thus non-endorsers share the belief that behavioral finance does not reflect decision behavior in fund manage-ment quite well (statement BF1). However, two groups may be distinguished with respect to statement BF2, i.e. their knowledge about behavioral

Three persons are not considered further in the analysis because they say to be convinced of behavioral finance (responding to BF1 with answering category 2) but have only limited knowledge about it (responding to BF2 with answering category 3 or 4).[12] Due to this definition based on answers to BF1 and BF2, the group of endorsers consists of 37 fund managers whereas the group of non-endorsers consists of 67 fund managers. Both groups are framed in the contingency table in Table 2.2.

As we aim for a comparison of endorsers with non-endorsers we use the descriptive items given in Table 2.1 in order to find out about differences in personal characteristics. Interestingly, the results in *Table 2.3* do not disclose any such difference to be statistically significant or even close to significance. Thus, the endorsement to behavioral finance is not closely related to personal characteristics, such as being older or holding a better position etc. In order to test the robustness of this result we also run a binary PROBIT regression where the variable "endorser versus non-endorser" is "explained" by available personal characteristics. The last two columns in Table 2.3 show that there is also no significant relation in this multivariate approach. As endorsers of behavioral finance do not represent a particular sub-group among fund managers, we do not control for personal characteristics in our further research.

---

finance. Splitting responses into those non-endorsers who know behavioral finance well (categories 1 and 2) and the others (categories 3 and more) gives groups with 32 and 35 fund managers, respectively. We have thus repeated all analyses with three groups (endorsers and two kinds of non-endorsers) in order to see whether the behavioral finance knowledge of non-endorsers may be a driving force in understanding them. But results remain almost unchanged and are thus robust in this respect. Only the level of significance is sometimes negatively affected by smaller sample size.

12 There are another seven fund managers who did not answer BF1 or BF2 in a useful way so that sample size is reduced from 114 to 107.

Table 2.3: Characteristics of endorsers and non-endorsers

Statements encoding in [ ]	Response category (a)	Responses			H_0: no difference (b)	Binary PROBIT regressions (c)	
		All fund managers	Endorsers	Non-endorsers			
Age in years <35 [1], 35-45 [3], >45 [5]	Mean N	*2.04* *114*	2.08 37	2.09 66	-0.031 (0.975)	-0.208 (0.281)	-0.151 (0.349)
Professional experience in years <5 [1], 5-15, [3], >15 [5]	Mean N	*2.89* *112*	3.00 34	2.82 67	-0.725 (0.468)	0.260 (0.158)	0.158 (0.285)
Gender male [1], female [2]	Mean N	*1.08* *115*	1.05 37	1.08 65	-0.437 (0.662)	1.019 (0.209)	0.150 (0.802)
Share variable compensation in %	Mean N	*25.78* *85*	28.35 30	25.53 49	-0.728 (0.467)	$7.62 * 10^{-5}$ (0.995)	-
University degree yes [1], no [2]	Mean N	*1.15* *112*	1.17 36	1.12 65	-0.604 (0.546)	0.211 (0.667)	0.213 (0.593)
Governing position yes [1], no [2]	Mean N	*1.62* *105*	1.63 30	1.63 64	-0.077 (0.938)	0.130 (0.745)	-
Kind of fund management (primarily) active [1], passive [2]	Mean N	*1.06* *110*	1.03 35	1.06 65	-0.718 (0.473)	-0.891 (0.305)	-0.603 (0.409)
Kind of securities managed stocks [1], bonds [2]	Mean N	*1.34* *114*	1.30 35	1.40 67	-0.986 (0.324)	-0.210 (0.556)	-0.233 (0.434)
R^2						0.062	0.024
[N]						67	93

(a) Responses in respective answering categories with analogical encoding in the first column.
(b) H_0 states that there is no difference between the groups of endorsers and non-endorsers. The figures given are the z-value of the Mann-Whitney U-test and the p-value in parentheses.
(c) The table gives the coefficient of the binary PROBIT regression and the p-value in parentheses.

Stars refer to level of significance: * 10%, ** 5%, *** 1%

2.3 Views on market's behavior

We ask fund managers to express their view on the behavior of other fund managers, i.e. the market, with respect to effects stated by behavioral finance. We find consistently that endorsers observe these effects significantly stronger than non-endorsers.

In order to systemize the variety of human behavioral biases Hirshleifer (2001) follows earlier studies of psychologists (see e.g. Alpert and Raiffa, 1982, Fischhoff, 1982b) and assigns biases either to the process of judgment or to the process of decision-making. Analogically, we ask for fund managers' response to statements [1] and [2], that serve to detect the judgment biases house money effect and confirmatory bias, and their response to statements [3]-[5] that rather describe the decision biases reflection effect, home bias and herding. *Table 2.4* presents the five statements we are analyzing and which we motivate in the following before going into results.

2.3.1 Motivation

Statement [1] in Table 2.4 addresses the *house money effect* caused by the mechanisms of heuristic simplification. Simplification becomes active because of the restraints in human information-processing capabilities due to which the complexity of the available basis of information is reduced by filtering out apparently irrelevant facts. By thus simplifying the information-input for decision-making perception of reality gets biased (Tversky and Kahneman, 1982). This can result in suboptimal decisions. In this context, house money effect describes the phenomenon that investors become less loss-averse and more likely to take risks when reinvesting recently made profits. The psychological explanation for this bias is that the perceived discomfort in case of a loss of the recently earned money is diminished by the fact that it was a gain before (Thaler and Johnson, 1990).

Statement [2] aims at the *confirmatory bias* which is attributed to the natural mechanism of self-deception. After a decision people tend to collect decision-confirming information thereby ignoring contrary evidence (Pronin, 2007). The confirmatory bias describes the observation that people are prone to interpret even ambiguous information in favor of their earlier decision. These natural mechanisms of selective information perception interfere with rational learning, including the recognition of and learning from one's own mistakes. The motivation for the confirmatory bias is to preserve self-respect of the decider as well as to avoid regret and thus unpleasant feelings after decision-making (Festinger, 1957, Nickerson, 1998).

Statements [3]-[5] mention decision biases. Statement [3] serves to detect the *reflection effect* (Kahneman and Tversky, 1979), grasped here by risk seeking behavior in case of loss positions. The reflection effect describes the dependence of investors' risk attitude on the sign of the outcome, i.e. whether the outcomes are gains or losses. It is included in prospect theory by the s-shape of the value function: concave for gains indicating risk aversion and convex for losses indicating risk seeking. This bias partly contributes to explain the disposition effect. The preference to invest in near located markets, the *home bias* (statement [4]), is explained – in the behavioral finance approach – by the human preference for familiarity, which evokes the feeling of possessing more relevant information about the home market and thus being more competent to forecast (Kilka and Weber, 2000, Lütje and Menkhoff, 2007). The third decision bias addressed here with statement [5] is *herding*. It is understood as the phenomenon that fund managers may imitate the investment decision of others and thereby ignore their own valuable information (see Bikhchandani and Sharma, 2001).

2.3.2 Results

Regarding the results in Table 2.4 we detect significant differences between endorsers and non-endorsers concerning the intensity of perception of biases in their colleagues' behavior and thereby in the market. This finding applies to the two judgmental biases, i.e. house money effect and confirmatory bias, and to the three decisional biases as well, i.e. reflection effect, home bias and herding.

In all five cases endorsers recognize the biases significantly stronger than non-endorsers, even though the latter mostly concede the existence of these behavioral finance effects too. Taking for example the house money effect (statement [1]), endorsers approve this with a mean answer of 2.59, whereas non-endorsers give a mean answer of 3.13 – indifference between approval and contradiction would occur at a value of 3.50. The difference between both groups is significant at the 5 percent level.[13]

---

13 As a referee notes, one may be concerned with the positive wording of statements in Table 4, as the observed tendency to agree with questions may reflect a bias in psychological measurement. However, this possibility is rather unlikely if one takes into account that these results do predict miscalibration and the choice of investment strategies in a meaningful way. Moreover, respondents rather deny the also positively worded sta-

Table 2.4: Assessment of other fund managers' behavior

[1] Statement: "After several profitable investments fund managers tend to take on additional positions".
[2] Statement: "My colleagues pay particular attention to confirmatory news/information after having made an investment decision".
[3] Statement: "In case of loss positions other fund managers tend to increase their willingness to take risks".
[4] Statement: "Fund managers prefer to invest in near located markets".
[5] Statement: "Also fund managers exhibit herding behavior".

Statements		Response category (a)	Responses			H_0: no difference (b)
			All fund managers	Endorsers	Non-endorsers	
[1]	*HOUSE MONEY EFFECT*	Mean	*2.92*	2.59	3.13	**-2.107**[**]
		N	*115*	37	67	**(0.035)**
[2]	*CONFIRMATORY BIAS*	Mean	*2.66*	2.35	2.91	**-2.483**[**]
		N	*115*	37	66	**(0.013)**
[3]	*REFLECTION EFFECT*	Mean	*3.44*	3.00	3.71	**-2.639**[***]
		N	*114*	37	65	**(0.008)**
[4]	*HOME BIAS*	Mean	*3.34*	3.03	3.54	**-1.745**[*]
		N	*116*	37	67	**(0.081)**
[5]	*HERDING*	Mean	*2.02*	1.81	2.19	**-1.841**[*]
		N	*116*	37	67	**(0.066)**

(a) There are six answering categories, ranging from "complete approval" (coded as 1) to "complete contradiction" (coded as 6). Thus, a mean of 3.5 or less indicates rather approval to the statement. N is the number of responses.
(b) H_0 states that there is no difference between the groups of endorsers and non-endorsers. The figures given are the z-value of the Mann-Whitney U-test and the p-value in parentheses.
Stars refer to level of significance: * 10%, ** 5%, *** 1%

Remarkably, the perception of herding is by far strongest compared to other biases. All fund managers agree with a mean of 2.02 to statement [5]. Again, the difference between both groups is statistically significant as endorsers perceive herding among fund managers stronger than non-endorsers.

The results in Table 2.4 indicate that the major fraction of professional fund managers observes behavioral finance effects in their daily working environment. This may be interesting in itself but our focus lies on the difference between the two groups distinguished: endorsers of behavioral

tement 9 in Table 5 below. Finally, our study primarily focuses on differences between two groups.

finance perceive these effects significantly stronger than non-endorsers. We are not aware that this result has been shown before, although it may confirm expectations. Against the background of this finding the next section examines the impact from endorsement of behavioral finance on fund managers' self-assessment. Will endorsers be able to control and quell their psychologically motivated biases to rationalize their behavior in order to optimize investment performance?

2.4 Views on one's own behavior

The view on one's own behavior provides a stunning contrast to the view on the market (see Section 2.3): we do not find any significant differences between endorsers and non-endorsers in our sample, with one exception, i.e. the issue of miscalibration.

The answers to the following five items provide pretty consistent results about fund managers' self-assessment. Just as for the view on markets, we follow psychologists and behavioral economists and distinguish the self-assessment items in those of judgment and decision-making (see *Table 2.5*). The first part of this section shortly motivates these items, the second part gives empirical results.

2.4.1 Motivation

We refer to judgment biases with statement [6], question [7] and task [8] which serve to analyze the three facets of overconfidence as they have been discussed in the literature, e.g. in Glaser and Weber (2007) and Menkhoff et al. (2006). Theory assumes that overconfidence often appears in situations with rare or ambiguous feedback (Lichtenstein et al., 1982, Hirshleifer, 2001). However, portfolio manager frequently get unmistakable feedback to their decisions and forecasts and they cannot establish themselves in the market with bad performance. In this context it seems plausible to expect that portfolio manger learn from their experience, thus being able to estimate the precision of their knowledge and abilities more adequate (Deaves et al., 2005). But, as indicated by the self-deception theory, the driving forces behind overconfidence may be stronger than rational learning. Many cognitive mechanisms distort an adequate self-assessment, thereby rather supporting overconfidence to keep self-esteem and respect of others after wrong decisions. Glaser et al. (2005) show in this respect that professional investors are even more overconfident than laymen in all the three interpretations of overconfidence.

The first dimension of overconfidence is the *illusion of control* (Langer, 1975) implying the following aspects: the belief of being able to control random variables, such as market trends, more than it is really possible, an unrealistic high estimation of one's own success probability as well as an exaggerated optimism concerning the future (Glaser and Weber, 2007). The psychological motivation for the illusion of control is the fact that people feel more comfortable in situations they can control. An aspect of this bias is the illusion of being able to explain events retrospectively which is also regarded as the origin of hindsight bias. Thus, we refer to overconfidence as illusion of control by statement [6]. Hindsight bias hinders an efficient information procession and derogates rational learning (Fischhoff, 1982a). Empirical studies show that despite the knowledge of its origins and effects, the hindsight bias cannot be easily reduced and that also professionals are subject to this bias (Fischhoff, 1982b, Biais and Weber, 2007).

One further facet of overconfidence is the unrealistically positive self-evaluation, the so-called *better-than-average-effect* (Taylor and Brown, 1988) which we address by question [7]. Especially concerning desirable skills people tend to estimate themselves above average. A prominent example for the better-than-average self-estimation is the study of Svenson (1981), in which 82 percent of participating students rank themselves to 30 percent of the safest drivers. Obviously, biased perception concerning one's own skills is in high gear. From one's own experience only others are subject to cognitive deception and behavioral biases. Thereby successes are referred to one's own abilities whereas failures are ascribed to external circumstances (Pronin et al., 2002, Pronin, 2007).

Finally, overconfidence is often regarded as *miscalibration* which we test by using task [8]. Miscalibration is a systematic overestimation of the precision of one's own knowledge. In consequence, people underestimate the probability distribution of a random variable (Lichtenstein et al., 1982, Alpert and Raiffa, 1982). Experimental psychology adopted the method of confidence intervals to measure miscalibration. Investors signalize their miscalibration by stating too narrow confidence intervals for estimations of stock or stock index developments.

In the following we refer to two decision biases. When approaching disposition effect and home bias that we have already touched to assess the market (Section 2.3), we do not rely on the same items for self-assessment in order to prevent strategic answers by respondents.

Over the past 20 years, the most commonly mentioned behavioral finance explanation for the *disposition effect* is the prospect theory view with its core messages: loss aversion and reflection effect (Kahneman and Tversky, 1979, Weber and Camerer, 1998, Langer and Weber, 2005). Accordingly, loss aversion is responsible for risk seeking in case of losses and consequently for the tendency to holding loss positions too long. This behavior is attributed to the hope that loser assets will rise or even outperform the actual winners in the future. Contrary, due to risk aversion in the domain of gains the realization of a secure profit is preferred to further holding a "winning" asset. This leads to selling winners too soon. Thus, investors change their risk attitude depending on the type of an outcome, the above elucidated reflection effect. Interestingly, Shefrin and Statman (1985) point out that prospect theory cannot explain the disposition effect by its own and consequently use several additional psychological elements besides prospect theory, i.e. mental accounting, regret aversion and self-control.[14] Recent research provides further doubt on the direct one-to-one link between prospect theory and disposition effect. Prospect theory does not always explain the disposition effect or does even predict opposite behavior (Barberis and Xiong, 2006, Hens and Vlcek, 2006). We approach the disposition effect by statement [9], thereby in particular concerning risk aversion in the domain of gains.[15]

Statement [10] refers to the *home bias* although with a different item than statement [4] from Table 2.4 above. We use the hypothetical question on international asset allocation here because fund managers are subject to restrictions of their clients who are not necessarily well informed about an optimal portfolio allocation or may be subject to regulation restricting international diversification. Thus, managed portfolios might differ from the ones preferred by the fund managers themselves. To avoid such a distortion, we ask fund managers for their personally preferred portfolio allocation, explicitly mentioning to ignore their funds' restrictions. According to the IAPM (International Asset Pricing Model) the optimal portfolio share of a country corresponds to the ratio of its market capitalization to world capitalization. German investors' portfolios should thus contain 4 percent of German stocks and 8 percent of German bonds (Lütje and Menkhoff, 2007).

For all three biases – overconfidence, disposition effect and home bias – there is clear evidence that they reduce risk-adjusted investment performance. In

---

14 We thank a referee for making us aware of this point.

15 The exact formulation relies on Odean's (1998, p. 1777) discussion of the disposition effect: "If the investor is faced with a liquidity demand, and has no new information about either stock, she is more likely to sell the stock that is up."

a series of studies the dismal effect of overconfidence has been revealed by Odean (1999), Biais et al. (2005), Biais and Weber (2007). Also Barber and Odean (2000, 2001) ascribe detrimental high trading activity to overconfidence.[16] Regarding the disposition effect, Odean (1998) discloses it as a source of suboptimal performance for individual investors. Shapira and Venezia (2001) find that both professionalism and experience diminish but do not eliminate the preference to realize profits too soon. A similar result is shown by Feng and Seasholes (2005): while sophistication and trading experience eliminate the reluctance to realize losses they only reduce but fail to eliminate the propensity to realize gains. Sluggish reaction due to the disposition effect may even generate stock price "underreaction" to corporate news (Frazzini, 2006). Accordingly, literature warns against the consequences of the disposition effect and proposes greater self-discipline as solution to reduce the costs of loss or regret aversion and relative unsuccessfulness (Coval and Shumway, 2005, Locke and Mann, 2005). Scherbina and Jin (2006) study the effect of replacements of mutual fund managers. They demonstrate that new fund managers sell the loser stocks they have inherited more readily, thus increasing future returns. Finally, there is evidence that international portfolio diversification may increase portfolio returns (depending of course on the benchmark country return) although emphasis is put on the advantage of international diversification due to imperfect return correlation between national markets (see Levy and Sarnat, 1970).

2.4.2 Results

We now turn to results which are presented in the main part of Table 2.5. Starting with the bias "illusion of control", is there any impact from being an endorser of behavioral finance on the degree of hindsight bias? By assessing statement [6] with a mean of 3.32 endorsers of behavioral finance find the majority of economic news slightly more surprising than non-endorsers (3.19). Illusion of control is not significantly lower for endorsers in this case although this tendency of information perception may seem desirable from the viewpoint of behavioral finance (as well as from the efficient market hypothesis). Thus, our result supports the persistence of the hindsight bias.

---

16 See Hilton (2007) for a more detailed discussion of overconfidence.

Table 2.5: Assessment of one's own behavior

[6] Statement: "The majority of economic news is not surprising for me".
[7] Question: "How do you evaluate your own performance compared to other asset managers?"
[8] Task: Give an estimation of the DAX in 1 month. Determine a lower und an upper bound such that the quote of the DAX in 1 month from now will be inside the resulting interval with a probability of 90%".
[9] Statement: "I prefer to take profits when I am confronted with unexpected liquidity demands".
[10] Task: Please, allocate an amount of 10 million € to the following markets so that the shares sum up to 100% (thereby ignore your funds' restrictions)". Germany, Europe (without Germany), USA and Canada, Asia, Emerging Markets.

Statements		Response category (a)	Responses			H_0: no difference (b)
			All fund managers	Endorsers	Non-endorsers	
[6]	*ILLUSION OF CONTROL (HINDSIGHT BIAS)*	Mean N	*3.20* *115*	3.32 36	3.19 67	-0.353 (0.724)
[7]	*BETTER-THAN-AVERAGE*	Mean N	*2.34* *111*	2.29 35	2.37 66	-0.621 (0.534)
[8]	*MISCALIBRATION*	Mean N	*887* *111*	1165 37	769 64	**-2.816***** **(0.005)**
[9]	*DISPOSITION EFFECT*	Mean N	*3.99* *116*	4.03 37	4.07 67	-0.014 (0.989)
[10]	*HOME BIAS (GERMANY)* (c)	Mean in % N	*14.21* *111*	14.60 36	14.30 64	-0.230 (0.818)

(a) There are six answering categories, ranging from "complete approval" (coded as 1) to "complete contradiction" (coded as 6). Thus, a mean of 3.5 or less indicates rather approval to the statement.

Statement 7: five answering categories: much better (coded as 1), slightly better (coded as 2), equally good (coded as 3), slightly worse (coded as 4), much worse (coded as 5). N is the number of responses.

(b) H_0 states that there is no difference between the groups of endorsers and non-endorsers. The figures given are the z-value of the Mann-Whitney U-test and the p-value in parentheses.

(c) Concerning the weighting of other countries there are also no significant differences between the groups.

Note: All managers' mean answer for statements [9] and [10] lies not between the means of the comparison groups due to adjustment of the group "endorsers" by three answers (Table 2.2).

Stars refer to level of significance: * 10%, ** 5%, *** 1%

Question [7] sheds light on overconfidence as unrealistically positive self-evaluation. In absence of overconfidence it is to expect that fund managers evaluate their own performance compared to that of their colleagues on average with 3, which is the coding for "equally good". The results in Table 2.5 show, however, that fund managers evaluate themselves by a mean of 2.34, thus clearly signaling overconfidence. The difference between endorsers and non-endorsers in this respect is negligible.

Task [8] serves to analyze the relation of miscalibration and the endorsement of behavioral finance. In this case respondents had to estimate a 90 percent confidence interval for the quote of Germany's main stock index DAX in one month ahead. Interestingly, endorsers state a significantly wider interval than non-endorsers (means of 1165 and 769 points respectively).[17] The share of correctly made forecasts is 66.7 percent in the group of endorsers and 47.2 percent in the group of non-endorsers. As the share of wrong estimations exceeds 10 percent we confirm miscalibration among professional fund managers in our sample (see e.g. Biais et al., 2005, Glaser et al., 2005) but show that miscalibration is significantly lower for endorsers of behavioral finance. This may be understood as successful learning by endorsers.

Turning to the disposition effect, i.e. statement [9], our groups do not differ in their assessment of the degree to be subject to the disposition effect themselves. They both rather deny it to hold too long on losing positions (means of 4.03 and 4.07 respectively). In contrast, they observe a related bias - the reflection effect- much clearer in the behavior of others (see Section 2.3, statement [3]).

Finally, also the result for statement [10] does not differ between our two groups. Both groups equally strongly overweigh the home country in their portfolios. This finding is contrasted by results on statement [4] in Table 2.4, whereupon home bias is observed in fund management.

All this raises the question why overconfidence as miscalibration seems to be a bias that is easier to overcome than other behavioral patterns? Psychologists claim that people want to think well of themselves and generally succeed in doing so, which is particularly difficult to overcome by learning when asking for a direct comparison between self versus others (Pronin et al., 2002, 2004). Hence, e.g. overconfidence as better-than-average effect or the denial of the disposition effect in one's own behavior can be regarded as consequence of the

---

17 Excluding the extreme 10% answers from the distribution, leaving the inner 90%, the Mann-Whitney U-test also shows a significant difference between the answers of the groups in the miscalibration task. The median in the group of endorsers is 760 points and 625 points in the group of non-endorsers.

wish to see oneself in a better light upon which the knowledge of these biases has no significant influence. The contrasting finding on the calibration task could thus be due to its formulation which does not directly ask to assess one's own skills as statements 6 and question 7 do. Therefore, this task might not activate the person-positivity bias, i.e. the affinity of individuals to assess themselves in far more positive terms than they assess most other people (Taylor and Brown, 1988). This could be the reason for why learning succeeds in the miscalibration task. Thus, if we regard the ambition to guard self-esteem as motivation to perform well in self-assessment, then in case of miscalibration endorsers of behavioral finance are, first, better informed how to attain a good result in this task, i.e. to forecast correctly, and, second, they are not (or less) hindered by cognitive self-esteem guarding mechanisms when answering this task. As a result, due to their greater awareness of miscalibration and the minor cognitive resistance to this task, endorsers state significantly wider (and thereby better) confidence intervals than non-endorsers.

In summary, we do not observe an impact of the endorsement of behavioral finance on one's own behavior. Rather, both groups – endorsers and non-endorsers – negate behavioral biases like the disposition effect in their own investment behavior. This creates a discrepancy between the view on the market and that on oneself, i.e. a clear disclosure of the bias blind spot. Thus, fund managers do not behave principally different from other people, despite their strong performance control and bonus incentives to rationalize behavior.[18] Thus, rational learning is difficult in case of self-perception (Ehrlinger et al., 2005) – here shown for fund managers.

2.5 Consequence on investment behavior

The purpose of this section is to analyze whether the endorsement to behavioral finance has any effect on practical investment behavior. As we find such effects, this serves as a credibility test of the bias blind spot – no impact on perception of own behavior – because endorsers obviously do behave differently in accordance with their conviction.

---

18 Pronin et al. (2002) as well as Ehrlinger et al. (2005) reveal for "normal" people that even with knowledge of the relevant biases their perception in the behavior of others is always stronger than their recognition in one's own behavior. Furthermore, test persons fail to agree to this biased self-perception and hold on to judge their self-assessment as objective and accurate.

In this section investment behavior is grasped by two items, addressing information sources and investment strategies. It is known in this respect that fund managers primarily base their decision on fundamental information (e.g. Menkhoff, 1998, Arnswald, 2001). However, due to the increasing recognition of behavioral effects on price formation in financial markets (DeBondt and Thaler, 1985; Jegadeesh and Titman, 2001; Barberis and Thaler, 2003; Shiller, 2003) the importance of non-fundamental information, such as technical analysis and technical trading strategies (e.g. momentum trading) may be even growing (early evidence in Grinblatt et al., 1995, Keim and Madhavan, 1995). Because of their stronger perception of behavioral anomalies in financial markets we expect endorsers trying toprofitably exploit the observed anomalies and thus to rely more on non-fundamental sources of information and investment strategies.

In detail, *Table 2.6* gives task [11] with the four important sources of information as revealed by fund managers in ex ante interviews. From the same set of interviews we derive most popular investment strategies as addressed by question [12] in *Table 2.7.*

Table 2.6 shows at first sight the superior role of fundamental facts as source of information for all fund managers. Compared to non-endorsers, the group of endorsers relatively stronger uses technical indicators (mean of 2.84 versus 3.26), whereby it assesses colleagues (mean of 3.38) and other market participants (mean of 3.93) as relatively less relevant sources of information. Even if these differences are not significant, the tendency to reject the no-difference hypothesis is relatively obvious in some cases, e.g. regarding the p-value of the Mann-Whitney U-Test of 0.125 for technical indicators. Colleagues and other market participants can be interpreted as sources of external confirmation for own decisions (Arnswald, 2001). Their relatively minor importance for endorsers might result from the fact that the latter relatively stronger perceive the behavior of other market participants as biased (Table 2.4). Therewith, the quality of these sources of information is lower for endorsers. In this sense their endorsement of behavioral finance has a recognizable influence, although it is not statistically significant.[19]

19 If we aggregate the four sources of information into a composite score (fundamental facts plus technical indicators minus colleagues minus other market participants) the difference between endorses and non-endorsers becomes significant (p-value of 0.054): compared to non-endorsers, endorsers assign relatively less importance to colleagues and other market participants than to fundamental facts and technical indicators.

Table 2.6: Assessment of information sources

[11] Task: "Please, assess the importance of the following sources of information for you". Answering categories: "Fundamental facts about the company / market", "Technical indicators", "Colleagues from the own company", "Other market participants, not from the own company".

Sources of information	Response category (a)	Responses			H_0: no difference (b)
		All fund managers	Endorsers	Non-endorsers	
Fundamental facts	Mean	*1.82*	1.86	1.87	-0.588
	N	*115*	37	67	(0.557)
Technical indicators	Mean	*3.02*	2.84	3.26	-1.533
	N	*114*	37	66	(0.125)
Colleagues	Mean	*3.17*	3.38	3.07	-1.147
	N	*115*	37	67	(0.251)
Other market participants	Mean	*3.73*	3.93	3.61	-1.258
	N	*115*	37	67	(0.208)

(a) There are 6 answering categories, ranging from "highest relevance" (coded as 1) to "no relevance" (coded as 6). N is the number of responses.
(b) H_0 states that there is no difference between the groups of endorsers and non-endorsers. The figures given are the z-value of the Mann-Whitney U-test and the p-value in parentheses.
Stars refer to level of significance: * 10%, ** 5%, *** 1%

Table 2.7 contains results about the use of the popular investment strategies in fund management. We see that the three main strategies as identified in interviews, i.e. buy-and-hold, momentum and contrarian trading, are of almost equal importance to our sample of fund managers. When we look at endorsers only, however, they prefer the technical trading strategies momentum and contrarian trading to a significantly higher degree than non-endorsers. This is consistent with their market assessment in Section 2.3 (Table 2.4) where they significantly stronger regard markets as being influenced by behavioral finance effects. In particular, the more intensive use of the momentum strategy seems plausible regarding the significantly stronger perception of herding in fund management (statement [5] in Table 2.4).

Table 2.7: Assessment of investment strategies

[12] Question: "How intensive do you use several strategies? Please, allocate 100%."
Answering categories:
"___% Momentum strategy", "___% Buy-and-Hold strategy",
"___% Contrarian strategy (Value strategy)", "___% Others"

Investment strategies	Response category (a)	Responses			H_0: no difference (b)
		All fund managers	Endorsers	Non-endorsers	
Momentum	Mean in %	*26.27*	29.49	23.92	**-2.033****
	N	*108*	36	62	**(0.042)**
Contrarian	Mean in %	*29.31*	34.28	26.96	**-2.395****
	N	*108*	36	62	**(0.017)**
Buy-and-hold (c)	Mean in %	*30.73*	23.54	32.96	-1.159
	N	*108*	36	62	(0.243)
Others	Mean in %	*13.69*	12.69	16.16	-0.113
	N	*108*	36	62	(0.910)

(a) N is the number of responses.
(b) H_0 states that there is no difference between the groups of endorsers and non-endorsers. The figures given are the z-value of the Mann-Whitney U-test and the p-value in parentheses.
(c) The standard deviation for the buy-and-hold strategy is much larger than that for momentum and contrarian strategies, which explains the insignificant difference of groups' answers in this case.
Stars refer to level of significance: * 10%, ** 5%, *** 1%

2.6 Conclusion

Recent empirical research in the field of behavioral finance has shown that professional investors are (just as well as private ones) subject to irrational, psychologically motivated biases in their investment decisions (e.g. Glaser et al., 2005, Haigh and List, 2005, Menkhoff et al., 2006). Even though professionalism may reduce biases to some degree it does not eliminate them entirely (Shapira and Venezia, 2001, 2006, Feng and Seasholes, 2005). This paper offers another perspective on the role of behavioral biases in finance by examining the impact from endorsement of behavioral finance on the perception of markets' and one's own behavior.

We provide evidence on this issue by examining survey data of more than 100 German fund managers. Distinguishing the respondents in two groups, endorsers and non-endorsers of behavioral finance, we test for differences in their answers with respect to perceived market-wide biases, self-assessment, information processing and investment strategies. Interestingly, there is no difference in personal characteristics between the two groups. Our findings show that the endorsement of behavioral finance has a significant impact on professionals' perception of markets, but that it hardly influences the view on one's own behavior. This finding holds although endorsers do behave differently from non-endorsers in the expected direction with respect to preferred information sources and investment strategies.

So far our findings clearly support the hypothesis that many behavioral biases are difficult to overcome by learning, even though the fund managers analyzed here have very strong incentives to learn efficient behavior. However, results do not only feed pessimism about the capabilities of financial professionals. One indication of learning is the significantly lower degree of miscalibration shown by endorsers. Moreover, their stronger reliance on technical analysis and trading strategies may not conform to expectations derived from the efficient market hypothesis; however, this behavior seems consistent with their endorsement of behavioral finance.

The results of our study demonstrate the persistence of behavioral patterns even with knowledge of their existence and thus their dominance over rational learning (in this sample). The failure to recognize own biases prevents from striving to correct them (Fischhoff, 1982b, Pronin, 2007). The challenge for professional fund managers, in particular for those with insight in behavioral finance, consists therefore in a more critical assessment of own investment behavior in order to discipline and rationalize it.

Appendix 1: Comparison of the sample with the industry's structure

	Structure of the German asset management industry:		
	- by assets under management		
Structure of data sample: - by assets under management	H_0: no difference [(b)] -0.325 (0.745)		
	- by company size [(b)]		
	Small player [12]	Medium player [24]	Big player [8]
- by company size	5	13	8
	H_0: no difference [(c)] 2.981 (0.225)		
Participation in the survey:	Pearson correlation coefficient with company size (by asset under management, p-value in parenthesis)		
- by number of questionnaires per company	0.472*** (0.001)		

The market data is based on the annual report of the German investment and asset management association (BVI) as of 2002.

(a) The table gives the z-value of the Mann-Whitney U-test with the p-value in parentheses.

(b) Here we focus on the company size of BVI member firms (ex those managing special funds only). The groups are clustered as follows: small players (mutual fund market share < 0.1%), medium players (mutual fund market share <= 2.5%), and big players (mutual fund market share > 2.5%) with numbers given in squared bracket.

(c) The table gives the test statistic of the chi-square test with the p-value in parenthesis.

Stars refer to level of significance: * 10%, ** 5%, *** 1%

3. Does training on behavioral finance influence fund managers'perception and behavior?[20]

3.1 Introduction

Psychologists argue that behavioral biases are difficult to overcome even with the knowledge of their existence (Pronin et al., 2002). From several studies we know that financial experts such as brokers, investment bankers or fund managers are subject to Behavioral Finance (BF) biases which negatively affect their performance (see e.g. Biais et al., 2005). As financial experts typically act fiduciarily, are monitored and paid for good performance, they, in fact, have stronger incentives to learn rational behavior. However, experts' sophistication and trading experience may diminish but still fail to eliminate biases such as e.g. the disposition effect (Shapira and Venezia, 2001, Feng and Seasholes, 2005, Visaltanachoti et al., 2007)[21]. Studies directly comparing the behavior of professionals and students unveil that professionals often behave even more overconfidently (Glaser et al., 2005) or exhibit a greater extent of myopic loss aversion than students (Haigh and List, 2005).

This paper ties up to the discussion on the persistence of behavioral anomalies in the behavior of financial professionals.[22] It analyzes the influence

---

20 This paper was originally published in Applied Financial Economics 20:7, 515-528, under the title "Does training on behavioural finance influence fund managers' perception and behaviour?" and is reproduced by kind permission of Taylor & Francis (Routledge). The Journal's web site is http://www.informaworld.com. I would like to thank all participating fund managers for their time and commitment. I thank Lukas Menkhoff, the participants of the Workshop Money, Banking, and Financial Markets in Düsseldorf and those of the Money Macro and Finance Research Group Conference in Bradford for their useful discussion. Moreover, I gratefully acknowledge the helpful comments of the anonymous referee and research assistance by Torsten Brozynski.

21 Shapira and Venezia (2001) detect that both professional and individual investors are subject to the disposition effect, whereas this effect is stronger for the latter. Feng and Seasholes (2005) show that sophistication and trading experience reduce the propensity to realize gains too soon, but fail to eliminate it. Visaltanachoti et al. (2007) provide strong evidence for the disposition effect in Chinese A-share markets, which are dominated by individual investors; however, regarding B-shares markets, which are dominated by sophisticated institutional investors, the evidence for the disposition effect is relatively weak.

22 Menkhoff and Nikiforow (2009) analyze the impact of fund managers' endorsement of behavioral finance on their perception of markets and themselves. This study reveals

of *training on BF* on professional fund managers' perception and investment behavior.[23] A questionnaire survey conducted among German fund managers provides data for this examination. First, the survey sample is split into two groups: (i) The "trained" fund managers, who get seminars and training on BF on the part of their employers, and the "untrained" ones, who do not get any training in that field. These two groups are tested for differences with respect to their perception of markets, their self-assessment as well as their choice of information sources and investment strategies. Second, apart from this general analysis, the underlying survey data allow for exploring two further interesting questions: (ii) How might "experts", i.e. those fund managers who assess themselves as possessing good knowledge in BF, differ from each other depending on whether they are trained in BF or not? (iii) How might "trained" fund managers differ from each other, depending on whether their company has integrated BF approaches into its investment processes or not?[24] These two additional considerations aim to examine the influence of training more specifically.

The analysis reveals that the degree of confrontation with BF in their daily business affects fund managers' perception and behavior in a different manner. *Training* on BF, which can be regarded as the weakest kind of implementation of BF issues, intensifies fund managers' perception of biases in the behavior of others, specifically the reflection effect and the home bias. Training also reduces the affinity to conformity – leading to less reliance on colleagues and other market participants as information sources; however, training does not result in a significant different reliance on other information sources regarded here, i.e. fundamental facts and technical indicators. *Integration* of BF into investment processes, regarded as strongest kind of implementation of BF, particularly influences fund managers' investment behavior. Regarding the information sources used, integration reduces the importance of fundamental facts (besides the importance of colleagues and other market participants). Furthermore, it significantly affects the use of investment strategies: The buy-and-hold strategy

---

that endorsers of behavioral finance significantly better recognize behavioral biases in the behavior of other fund managers. However, the view of one's own biases is hardly influenced by the endorsement of behavioral finance. Thus, even though endorsers of behavioral finance are well-informed about the existing behavioral biases and have strong incentives to learn efficient behavior, they still fail to recognize their own biases more appropriately. Such a biased self-perception might hinder the effort to overcome one´s own biases.

23 Henceforth, "training" stands for "training on behavioral finance".

24 Henceforth, "integration" or "integration of behavioral finance approaches" stands for "integration of behavioral finance approaches into investment processes of a company".

loses its relevance mostly in favor of other strategies (an answering category not specified in the survey, but different to the strategies momentum, contrarian, and buy-and-hold) as well as in favor of the behavioral-finance-motivated momentum strategy. Hence, training alone rather influences fund managers' perception and only partly their investment behavior (at least with regard to the information sources used), whereas the latter is mainly affected by integration of BF approaches into investment processes.[25]

The remainder of this paper is structured as follows. Section 3.2 describes the data of the questionnaire survey. The comparison groups for the three analyses are defined in Section 3.3. Section 3.4 presents the results regarding the groups' perception, specifically that of markets and themselves. Section 3.5 focuses on the effects on groups' investment behavior. Section 3.6 concludes the paper.

3.2 Data

Between August 15 and December 12, 2002 we conducted a questionnaire survey in Germany which yielded a representative sample of 117 questionnaires from 35 relevant German fund management companies. Concerning participating fund management companies - out of the 59 fund management companies we addressed - this survey resulted in a response rate of 59%. To avoid any misinterpretation in the formulation of questions and thus to ensure the reliability of responses, many intensive interviews with fund managers as well as pre-tests were held before starting the survey. Feedback indicates that the response is useful for our research purpose.[26]

---

25 We regard the non-influence of training on fund managers' investment behaviour as a result of an investment process being determined not by fund managers themselves but by others, e.g. by a company's senior management and/or the head of an asset management team. Thus, fund managers usually have to follow some given investment guidelines, without having a direct influence on them. In this case the given investment guidelines represent a kind of an institutional "barrier", which hinders fund managers from adjusting their investment approach to their knowledge of behavioral finance. This is a plausible explanation for the observed non-influence of training on fund managers' investment behaviour. In contrast, the impact of training becomes observable when fund managers are not restricted by anything, i.e. in case of their perception.

26 The analyses in Menkhoff and Schmidt (2005) and Menkhoff et al. (2006) rely on the same survey.

Table 3.1: Familiarity with behavioral finance [BF]: Training, knowledge, integration [(a)]

[BF1] Statement: "My employer provides in-house training on behavioral finance or sends his/her employees to appropriate seminars".

[BF2] Statement: "I've already concerned myself with behavioral finance, the key messages are well known to me".

[BF3] Statement: "Behavioral finance approaches are already integrated in the investment process of our company".

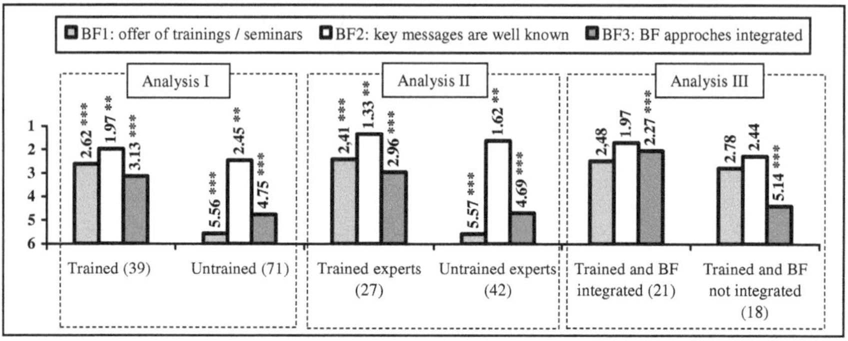

		H₀: No difference (b)		
Statements	*All fund managers (mean and number of responses)*	Analysis I	Analysis II	Analysis III
BF1: offer of training and seminars	*4.52* *110*	**-8.988***** **(0.000)**	**-7.207***** **(0.000)**	-0.893 (0.372)
BF2: key messages are well known	*2.42* *116*	**-2.111**** **(0.035)**	**-2.300**** **(0.021)**	-1.590 (0.112)
BF3: BF approaches are integrated	*4.17* *110*	**-5.144***** **(0.000)**	**-4.091***** **(0.000)**	**-5.477***** **(0.000)**

(a) The diagram gives the mean answers of the respective group (with the number of responses in parentheses) to the respective statements. Each statement can be assessed by six answering categories, shown on the y-axis, ranging from "completely agree" (coded as 1) to "completely disagree" (coded as 6). Thus, a mean of 3.5 or less indicates rather approval to the statement.

(a) H_0 states that there is no difference between the respective comparison groups. The figures given are the z-value of the Mann-Whitney U-test and the p-value in parentheses.

Stars refer to level of significance: * 10%, ** 5%, *** 1%

To analyze, first, the influence of training on BF as well as, second, the influence of the integration of BF findings into the investment process on fund managers' perception and investment behavior, three pairs of comparison groups are considered. These groups are formed by reverting to three statements in the questionnaire. These statements are given in *Table 3.1* as [BF1], [BF2], and [BF3], all assessed by six answering categories, ranging from "completely agree" (coded as 1) to "completely disagree" (coded as 6). By the degree of approval to statement [BF1], the respondent expresses to which extent he or she is trained on BF. For a more specific differentiation, the information from statement [BF2] is also used, where fund managers assess their state of knowledge in BF. By assessing statement BF3, the respondent states to which extent his or her company implements BF findings in its investment process.

3.3 Formation of comparison groups

3.3.1 "Trained" versus "Untrained" fund managers (analysis I)

The analysis starts by considering the general influence of *training* on BF on fund managers' perception and behavior. For this purpose, the respondents are split into two comparison groups based on their assessment of statement [BF1], asking about the offer of training and seminars on the part of the respondent's employer.

Figure 3.1: "Trained" versus "Untrained" fund managers (analysis I)

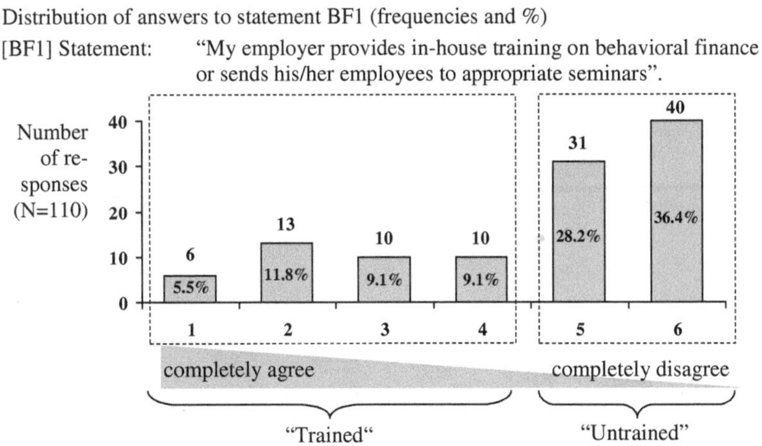

Regarding the answer distribution to statement [BF1] in *Figure 1*, it becomes obvious that BF still plays an inferior role in German fund management companies. Only 6 of 110 (5.5%) respondents get relatively intensive training on BF issues (answering category "completely agree" coded as 1), whereas 40 of them (36.4%) get no offer for BF education or training at all (answering category "completely disagree" coded as 6).

Due to the striking left-skewed distribution of answers, it seems plausible to define those fund managers with answering categories 1-4 as "trained" ones and assign those with answering categories 5-6 to the "untrained" group. This way of clustering results in 39 trained (35.5%) versus 71 untrained (64.5%) fund managers.

3.3.2 "Trained experts" versus "Untrained experts" (analysis II)

According to the chi-square test as well as to the Spearman rank correlation, the statements [BF1] and [BF2] are not independent.[27] Their significant positive correlation (p-value 0.015) implies that the knowledge of BF key messages improves with an increasing offer of seminars to BF, which is not really surprising but rather expected. This confirmation of the expected relation between [BF1] and [BF2] provides a good basis for the second, more specific analysis, i.e. whether it matters to be a trained or an untrained "expert" in BF *(Table 3.2)*. Focusing only on "experts", i.e. those fund managers who possess *"good knowledge" in BF*, might reveal a specific, marginal influence of training on this good knowledge: As "trained experts" regularly stay in touch with recent insights into BF research, one might expect that their knowledge is frequently updated and their behavior rather well trained in this field.

27 The result of the chi-square test for statements BF1 and BF2 is 30.602 with the p-value 0.061. The coefficient of the Spearman rank correlation is 0.232 with the p-value 0.015.

Table 3.2: "Trained experts" versus "Untrained experts" (analysis II)

[BF1] Statement: "My employer provides in-house training on behavioral finance or sends his/her employees to appropriate seminars".

[BF2] Statement: "I've already concerned myself with behavioral finance, the key messages are well known to me".

		Distribution of responses (frequencies)							
		BF1: Employer provides training and seminars on behavioral finance (completly agree … completely disagree)							
		1	**2**	**3**	**4**	**5**	**6**	Σ	
BF2: Key messages of behavioral finance are well known to the respondent	**1**	6	4	5	3	8	8	*34*	"Experts"
	2	0	6	0	3	10	16	*35*	"Experts"
	3	0	3	2	2	7	8	*22*	"No experts"
	4	0	0	3	2	5	4	*14*	"No experts"
	5	0	0	0	0	1	4	*5*	"No experts"
	6	-	-	-	-	-	-		"No experts"
	Σ	*6*	*13*	*10*	*10*	*31*	*40*	*110*	
		"Trained" (1–4)				"Untrained" (5–6)			

In contrast, the "untrained experts" might have gained their good knowledge of BF in seminars or training some time ago or even through self-study. Therefore, compared to the trained experts, the untrained experts do not stay in touch with BF issues so regularly, so that they can be assumed to be relatively less sophisticated regarding BF issues. As this second analysis aims for a more specific differentiation of groups, it can also be regarded as a robustness test for the first analysis.

To analyze whether it matters to be a trained or an untrained expert, the information from the assessment of availability of training on BF [BF1] is combined with the information on the state of knowledge in BF [BF2]. First, "experts" in BF are defined as those fund managers who assess themselves as possessing "good knowledge" of the BF key messages, i.e. who answer statement [BF2] with answering categories 1 and 2.[28] Second, the group of experts is differentiated according to their assessment of statement [BF1]. This consideration results in 27 "trained experts", who posses good knowledge of BF

28 Due to the distribution of answers to statement BF2 (see the contingency table in Table 1) the group "experts" is defined by comprising answering categories 1 and 2, whereas category 3 seems to characterize an intermediate stance in comparison to the sample.

due to training (BF1-answering categories 1-4), and 42 "untrained experts", who posses good knowledge without training (BF1-answering categories 5-6). These two groups are framed in the contingency table in Table 3.2.

3.3.3 "Trained and BF integrated" versus "Trained and BF not integrated" (analysis III)

The third analysis examines whether "trained" fund managers' differ among themselves depending on the *extent of integration* of BF approaches into investment processes of their company. Thus, it tests for additional influences on trained fund managers emerging particularly from the integration of BF. The contingency table in *Table 3.3* illustrates the definition of the comparison groups for this analysis.

Table 3.3: "Trained and BF integrated" versus "Trained and BF not integrated" (analysis III)

[BF1] Statement: "My employer provides in-house training on behavioral finance or sends his/her employees to appropriate seminars".

[BF3] Statement: "Behavioral finance approaches are already integrated in the investment process of our company".

Distribution of responses (frequencies)									
		BF1: Employer provides training and seminars on behavioral finance (completely agree – completely disagree)							
		1	**2**	**3**	**4**	**5**	**6**	Σ	
BF3: Behavioral finance approaches are integrated into investment process	**1**	4	2	0	1	1	1	*9*	"BF integrated"
	2	1	1	2	2	2	1	*9*	"BF integrated"
	3	1	3	0	4	7	4	*19*	"BF integrated"
	4	0	5	6	2	4	3	*20*	"BF not integrated"
	5	0	2	0	1	11	9	*23*	"BF not integrated"
	6	0	0	2	0	6	22	*30*	
	Σ	*6*	*13*	*10*	*10*	*31*	*40*	*110*	
		"Trained"				"Untrained"			

The focus is put only on "trained" fund managers as defined in Section 3.3.1. Here, this group is further separated on the basis of answers to statement [BF3], asking about the extent to which the respondent's company implements BF findings in its investment process. Regarding the distribution of answers for [BF3] given in Table 3.2, the comparison groups are formed by comprising the [BF3] answering categories 1-3 vs. 4-6. This defines the groups "Trained and BF integrated" with 21 fund managers, and "Trained and BF not integrated" with 18 fund managers.

3.4 Trained fund mangers' perception of markets and their self-assessment

3.4.1 Perception of markets

To learn about fund managers' perception of markets, we ask them to assess the five statements given in *Table 3.4*.

The *house money effect*, which is grasped by the statement Market Perception 1 [MP1], names the phenomenon that investors become less loss-averse and more likely to take risks when reinvesting recently made profits. Psychologically, this behavior is explained through the fact that the perceived discomfort in case of a loss of recently earned money is diminished only because it was a gain before (Thaler and Johnson, 1990).

The *confirmatory bias* (statement [MP2]) describes a behavioral propensity which occurs after a decision has been made. Then, people tend to collect information which confirms their decisions, thereby ignoring contrary evidence or interpreting even ambiguous information in favor of their earlier decision. The confirmatory bias serves to preserve the self-respect of a decider as well as to avoid regret or unpleasant feelings after decision-making (Festinger, 1957, Nickerson, 1998, Pronin, 2007).

Statement [MP3] addresses the *reflection effect*. This behavioral bias implies a change in the risk attitude of an investor depending on whether an outcome is a gain or a loss: People display risk aversion in the domain of gains, whereas they behave loss averse and even risk seeking in the domain of losses (Kahneman and Tversky, 1979). Statement [MP3] asks about the risk seeking behavior in case of loss positions, which partly explains the disposition effect[29], subsuming that investors tend to hold loser assets too long.

---

29 Investors' propensity to hold loser stocks too long and to sell winner stocks too early was called the "disposition effect" by Shefrin and Statman (1985).

Statement [MP4] serves to detect the *home bias*, i.e. the preference to invest in the home market or in markets in closer proximity. The psychological explanation for this bias is the human preference for familiarity, associated with the belief that one possesses more or even special information about the local market (Babilis and Fitzgerald, 2005, Konishi, 2007, Lütje and Menkhoff, 2007).[30]

Herding is the last BF bias considered here with statement [MP5]. Herding means that - under certain circumstances - fund managers imitate the behavior of others, thereby ignoring their own relevant information (see Bikhchandani and Sharma, 2001, Guo and Shih, 2008, Lütje, 2008).[31]

Results

Table 3.4 gives the mean answers of the respective group to the statements [MP1]-[MP5]. Regarding the formation of the bars it is striking that, except for the reflection effect (statement [MP3]), the perception intensities for the five biases examined here are rather equally ranked in all groups: Herding [MP5] is perceived most strongly, followed by the confirmatory bias [MP2], the house money effect [MP1] and finally the home bias [MP4]. A significant impact of training on the perception of biases in the market is observable in the case of the *reflection effect* [MP3] in analyses I and II. Trained fund managers perceive this bias significantly more strongly than the untrained ones (mean of 3.08 versus 3.64). Trained experts among the fund managers shape up as being mostly sensitized to this bias (mean of 2.88) which partly accounts for the well-known disposition effect. This result indicates a learning effect and thus an obvious impact of training on fund managers' market perception.

30 In the UK pension fund portfolios, Babilis and Fitzgerald (2005) detect strong evidence for the home bias against overseas foreign assets, and among the latter, in particular, against emerging markets. In the German market, the study of Lütje and Menkhoff (2007) reveals the home bias in the behavior of professional equity managers. Konishi (2007) provides some evidence for the reduction of the home bias when the world stock markets are integrated, thus giving foreign investors the opportunity of investing in domestic stocks more easily (here shown for NASDAQ).

31 For the Taiwan market Guo and Shih (2008) show that the degree of directional comovement, as a modified measure of herd behaviour, is higher in the high-tech stocks market than in traditional industries. Furthermore, they find that herding is greater during extreme up markets for all industries. Lütje (2009) provides evidence for reputational herding among professional fund managers. In his study, herding managers regard themselves as generally more risk averse than their non-herding peers.

Table 3.4: Market perception [(a)] [MP]

[MP1] Statement: "After several profitable investments fund managers tend to take on additional positions".
[MP2] Statement: "My colleagues pay particular attention to confirmatory news / information after having made an investment decision".
[MP3] Statement: "In case of loss positions other fund managers tend to increase their willingness to take risks".
[MP4] Statement: "Fund managers prefer to invest in near located markets".
[MP5] Statement: "Also fund managers exhibit herding behavior".

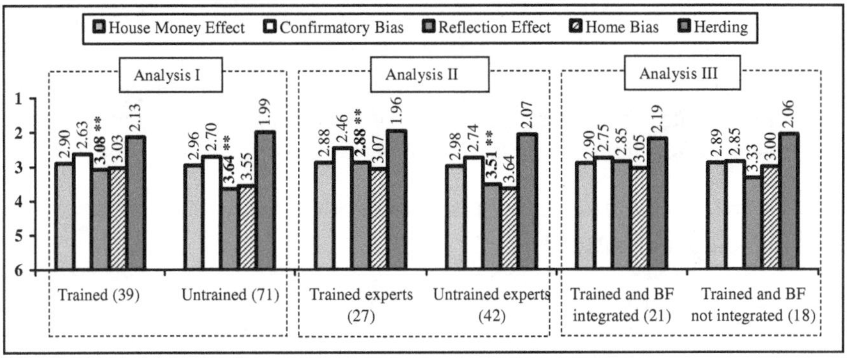

S

Statements	*All fund managers (mean and number of responses)*	H$_0$: No difference [(b)]		
		Analysis I	Analysis II	Analysis III
[1] House money effect	*2.92*	-0.124	-0.359	-0.236
	115	(0.901)	(0.720)	(0.814)
[2] Confirmatory bias	*2.66*	-0.137	-0.832	-0.718
	115	(0.891)	(0.406)	(0.473)
[3] Reflection effect	*3.44*	**-2.123****	**-1.939***	-1.551
	114	**(0.034)**	**(0.052)**	(0.121)
[4] Home bias	*3.34*	-1.626	-1.423	-0.377
	116	(0.104)	(0.155)	(0.706)
[5] Herding	*2.02*	-1.436	-0.127	-0.445
	116	(0.151)	(0.899)	(0.656)

(a) The diagram gives the mean answers of the respective group (with the number of responses in parentheses) to the respective statements. Each statement can be assessed by six answering categories, shown on the y-axis, ranging from "completely agree" (coded as 1) to "completely disagree" (coded as 6). Thus, a mean of 3.5 or less indicates rather approval to the statement.

(b) H$_0$ states that there is no difference between the respective comparison groups. The figures given are the z-value of the Mann-Whitney U-test and the p-value in parentheses.

Stars refer to level of significance: * 10%, ** 5%, *** 1%

In particular, an increased awareness of the reflection effect is a very welcome result, considering that the literature warns against the consequences of the disposition effect, for which several studies provide evidence of its negative impact on risk-adjusted performance (Odean, 1998, Coval and Shumway, 2005, Locke and Mann, 2005).

Furthermore, the difference in the perception of the *home bias* in analysis I is close to significance (p-value of 0.104): Compared to untrained fund managers, the trained ones observe the home bias remarkably more strongly (mean of 3.03 versus 3.55). In analysis II, this difference also persists among the experts on BF with a p-value of 0.155.

Analysis III does not reveal any significant results. Thus, integration of BF approaches into investment processes of a company does not seem to additionally affect trained fund managers' perception of markets

3.4.2 Self-assessment

This section focuses on fund *managers' perception of their own behavior. Table 3.5* documents the groups' answers to the following five items. Statement Self-Assessment 1 [SA1], question [SA2], and task [SA3] refer to the three facets of overconfidence: *Illusion of control* (Langer, 1975), grasped here by the persistent *hindsight bias* (Biais and Weber, 2007), *better-than-average effect* (Taylor and Brown, 1988) as well as *miscalibration* (Lichtenstein et al., 1982). For further discussion on these three interpretations of overconfidence, see e.g. Menkhoff et al. (2006) and Glaser and Weber (2007). Statement [SA4] addresses another driving force of the *disposition effect*: As a counterpart to the assessment of their peers' behavior in the domain of losses (statement [MP3] Section 3.4.1), the surveyed fund managers are now asked to comment their own *risk aversion* in the domain of gains. This phenomenon also motivates the preference to sell "winning" assets too soon (Kahneman and Tversky, 1979, Shefrin and Statman, 1985, Weber and Camerer, 1998). Statement [SA5] aims to assess fund managers' *affinity to conformity*, also regarded as a motivation for herding (Bikhchandani and Sharma, 2001).

All these biases are guided by emotions and other natural human mechanisms preserving self-esteem and avoiding cognitive dissonance of the decision-maker. These mechanisms interfere with rational learning, including the recognition of and learning from one's own mistakes (Hirshleifer, 2001). Several studies have shown that the biases analyzed in this section have a negative impact on risk-adjusted investment performance (see Odean, 1999,

Barber and Odean, 2000, 2001, Coval and Shumway, 2005, Biais and Weber, 2007). What will be the influence of training and integration of BF on fund managers' self-assessment and thus their ability to regard their own behavioral biases more critically?

Results

The only significant result in Table 3.5 reveals that training on BF significantly diminishes the *affinity to conformity* (statement [SA5]). In analysis I, there is a significantly stronger denial by trained fund managers that the discussion of an investment decision with colleagues reduces the pressure to succeed (means of 4.28 versus 3.58 with a p-value of 0.022). In the group of experts in analysis II, this result sustains with a lower level of significance (means of 4.37 versus 3.74 with a p-value of 0.096). This attitude in the group of trained fund managers might result from the knowledge of social psychology that, in contrast to the idea of the perfect group decision, where the group's members offset each other's biases, groups in fact reduce the variance of their members' opinions in a decision-making process. Thus, discussions of an investment decision in groups rather provide a feeling of confidence, conformity and competence (especially when one's own view is consistent with the view of the group) than result in better solutions (Montier, 2005). In that context, we might conclude that training does have a significant impact on the recognition that group-based consensus decisions do not necessarily lead to the best decision making as they reduce group members' variance of views, thereby lowering their creativity. The self-perception of all the other biases (mentioned in Table 3.5) turns out to be not significantly affected by training.

Table 3.5: Self-assessment [(a)] [SA]

[SA1] Statement: "The majority of economic news is not surprising for me".
[SA2] Question: "How do you evaluate your own performance compared to other asset managers?"
[SA3] Task[(c)]: "Give an estimation of the DAX in one month. Determine a lower und an upper bound such that the quote of the DAX in one month from now will be inside the resulting interval with a probability of 90%".
[SA4] Statement: "I prefer to take profits when I am confronted with unexpected liquidity demands".
[SA5] Statement: "Discussion of an investment decision with colleagues reduces the pressure to succeed".

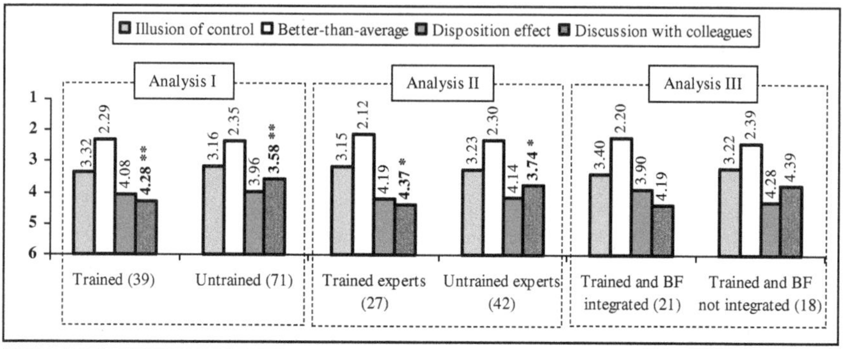

Statements	*All fund managers (mean and number of responses)*	H_0: No difference [(b)]		
		Analysis I	Analysis II	Analysis III
[SA1] Illusion of control (Hindsight bias)	*3.20* *115*	-0.780 (0.436)	-0.183 (0.855)	-0.623 (0.533)
[SA2] Better-than-average	*2.34* *111*	-0.695 (0.487)	-0.280 (0.201)	-0.515 (0.614)
[SA3] Miscalibration [(c)]	*887* *111*	-0.649 (0.516)	-0.870 (0.384)	-1.536 (0.124)
[SA4] Disposition effect	*3.99* *116*	-0.529 (0.597)	-0.151 (0.880)	-0.546 (0.585)
[SA5] Affinity to conformity	*3.73* *116*	**-2.295**** **(0.022)**	**-1.665*** **(0.096)**	-0.519 (0.604)

(a) The diagram gives the mean answers of the respective group (with the number of responses in parentheses) to the respective statements. Each statement, except statement [SA2], can be assessed by six answering categories, shown on the y-axis, ranging from "completely agree" (coded as 1) to "completely disagree" (coded as 6). Thus, a mean of 3.5 or less indicates rather approval to the statement. For statement [SA2] there are five answering categories: much better (coded as 1), slightly better (coded as 2), equally good (coded as 3), slightly worse (coded as 4), much worse (coded as 5).

(b) H_0 states that there is no difference between the respective comparison groups. The figures given are the z-value of the Mann-Whitney U-test and the p-value in parentheses.

(c) The results for task [SA3] are not given in the diagram. The means for the stated interval are 945 vs. 878 for analysis I, 1074 vs. 896 for analysis II, and 800 vs. 600 for analysis III.

Stars refer to level of significance: * 10%, ** 5%, *** 1%

Table 3.6 additionally presents the results for the *home bias* task in the questionnaire. This task serves to analyze whether training on BF affects fund managers' skills to diversify their portfolios internationally in an appropriate manner or whether fund managers remain prone to overweighting German assets (their home market) in their portfolios. The latter result would confirm the findings of several studies indicating the persistence of the home bias (Lütje and Menkhoff, 2007, Solnik, 2007). To obtain fund managers' personally preferred portfolios, which might differ from their managed ones due to restrictions e.g. on the part of their clients, task [AA] asks them to allocate a hypothetical amount of 10 million € to the global financial markets, thereby ignoring the respective fund's restrictions.

According to the International Asset Pricing Model (IAPM), the optimum portfolio share of a country corresponds to the ratio of its market capitalization to the world capitalization. German investors' portfolios should thus contain 4% of German stocks and 8% of German bonds.[32]

Even with the explicit hint to ignore their funds' restrictions in this task, all the groups equally strongly overweight their home country Germany in their portfolios (around 14%). However, compared to the mean allocation of the whole sample as well as to analysis I, analyses II and III detect a shift in the allocation from Europe towards the USA and Canada. Compared to the untrained experts, trained experts (analysis II) would invest significantly more in the USA and Canada (mean of 34.28% versus 28.70%), thereby decreasing their European engagements (30.90% versus 35.22%). This tendency is also shown in analysis III: The group "Trained and BF integrated" differs from its comparison group by a remarkably lower investment share in Europe (means of 30.91% versus 36.94% with a p-value of 0.172), mainly investing in the USA and Canada (35.32% versus 29.89% with a p-value of 0.254).

32 Regarding this home bias task, it should be noted that specific overweightings of countries could also reflect active fund managers' market opinions (i.e. tracking error vs. neutral market weighting), even if they are well aware of the neutral, well diversified portfolio (according to global benchmarks).

Table 3.6: International asset allocation [(a)] [AA]

[AA] Task: "Please allocate an amount of 10 million € to the following markets so that the shares sum up to 100% (thereby ignoring your funds' restrictions)."

__% Germany __% Europe (without Germany)__% USA and Canada"

__% Asia __% Emerging Markets.

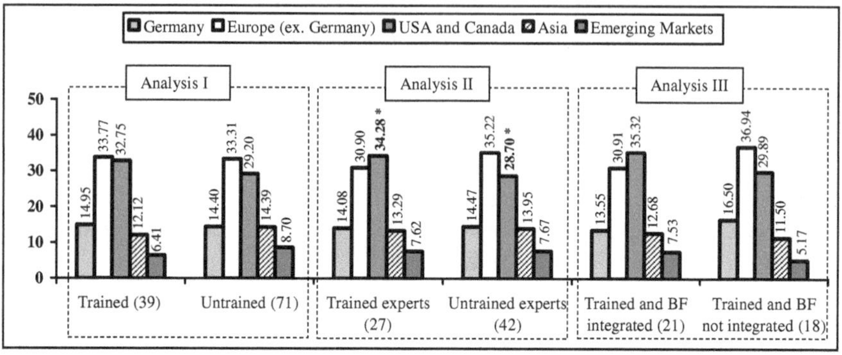

		H_0: No difference [(b)]		
Statements	*All fund managers (mean and number of responses)*	Analysis I	Analysis II	Analysis III
Germany	*14.21* *111*	-0.144 (0.886)	-0.102 (0.913)	-0.744 (0.457)
Europe (without Germany)	*33.68* *111*	-0.429 (0.668)	-0.834 (0.404)	-1.366 (0.172)
USA and Canada	*30.61* *111*	-1.301 (0.193)	**-1.720*** **(0.086)**	-1.140 (0.254)
Asia	*13.62* *111*	-0.459 (0.646)	-0.433 (0.665)	-0.317 (0.752)
Emerging Markets	*7.89* *111*	-1.329 (0.184)	-0.063 (0.950)	-1.374 (0.169)

(a) The diagram gives the mean answers of the respective group (with the number of responses) in %.

(b) H_0 states that there is no difference between the respective comparison groups. The figures given are the z-value of the Mann-Whitney U-test and the p-value in parentheses.

Stars refer to level of significance: * 10%, ** 5%, *** 1%

Regarding these analyses, training seems not to affect the exaggerated preference to invest in the German home market, which supports the persistence of the home bias as reported in the literature. However, if we widen the definition for the "home market" from Germany to Europe, the picture changes. The observed tendencies of shifting the main investment share from the European market to a more highly capitalized American market (see analyses II and III) might be interpreted as an effort to overcome the concentration on the European home market. This conclusion would hold for 25% of the sample. Thus, in the case of experts, training significantly contributes to diminishing their home bias on the European level, whereas the investment share for the German home market remains at the same (overweighted) level. Also, fund managers working in companies that implement BF approaches show rather more effort in struggling against the European home bias.

In summary, the main results of Section 3.4 are the following. First, with respect to fund managers' perception of markets, training on BF contributes to a significant better recognition of the reflection effect. Second, also the perception of the home bias becomes remarkably improved. Third, when it comes to self-assessment, training results in a significantly lower affinity to discussing decisions in groups and thus in a lower affinity to conformity, implying a lower tendency to imitate the decisions of others. Fourth, the diversification task reveals that trained experts would allocate a significantly higher share of assets to the USA and Canada, thereby shifting the weighting from the closer European markets. By the same token, the group "Trained and BF integrated" tends to allocate less investment to Europe.

Thus, the results of Section 3.4 detect some influence of training on fund managers' perception of markets and themselves. These influences might be understood as a learning process towards a more rational behavior, which training in BF aims to activate. However, it is not observable that trained fund managers' perception is additionally (significantly) affected by the integration of BF approaches into investment processes.

3.5 Consequences on the investment behavior

After focusing on fund managers' perception, next, their *investment behavior* is examined. Again, the analysis differentiates whether fund managers are trained on BF issues or not as well as whether they work in companies with integrated BF approaches or not.

Within the survey, investment behavior is grasped through the choice of information sources and investment strategies. The four sources of information given in *Table 3.7*, as well as the four investment strategies presented in *Table 3.8*, have been named as important for the investment management by fund managers in ex-ante interviews.[33]

According to analysis I in Table 3.7, training does not significantly affect the ranking in the use of information sources: Fundamental facts turn out to be the main information source, followed by technical indicators, colleagues[34] and finally by other market participants. Compared to the untrained fund managers, the trained ones tend to assess colleagues and other market participants as relatively less important (analysis I). This difference becomes significant in analysis II: Compared to the untrained experts, trained experts rely significantly less on their colleagues (means of 3.41 versus 2.81) and other market participants (4.02 versus 3.52).[35] This assessment is absolutely consistent with trained experts' lower affinity to conformity, detected by the results from statement [SA5] in Table 3.5. Thus, less affinity to conformity seems to result in a lower consideration of colleagues and other market participants as information sources.[36] One plausible implication of this finding might be that trained experts more strongly trust in their own information. This might lead to a higher independence in their information processing, resulting in decisions being relatively less susceptible to market noise.

Analysis III in Table 3.7 reveals some first significant influences of the integration of BF approaches into investment processes. Compared to the untrained fund managers, trained fund managers in firms which implemented BF approaches attach significantly less importance to fundamental facts (mean of 2.26 versus 1.56), colleagues (3.76 versus 2.89) and other market participants (4.36 versus 3.44) as information sources.

---

33 Menkhoff and Schmidt (2005) find that the strategies buy-&-hold, momentum and contrarian are typically applied mutually. Their use reflects the viewpoints and the level of risk-aversion of the respective fund manager.

34 In the questionnaire this source of information is given as "Colleagues in the own company". In our pretest interviews fund managers indicated that they regard this answering category as a generic one, including their colleagues' statements/analyses/opinions.

35 To assess the relevance of the information sources given in the questionnaire there are 6 answering categories, ranging from "highest relevance" (coded as 1) to "no relevance" (coded as 6).

36 Arnswald (2001) explains the importance assigned to these sources of information by interpreting them as a kind of external confirmation of one's own decisions. But he also mentions them to be channels for contagions of fear and exuberance.

Table 3.7: Assessment of information sources [(a)] *[INFO]*

[INFO] Task: "Please assess the importance of the following sources of information for you". "Fundamental facts about the company / market", "Technical indicators", "Colleagues from the own company", "Other market participants, not from the own company".

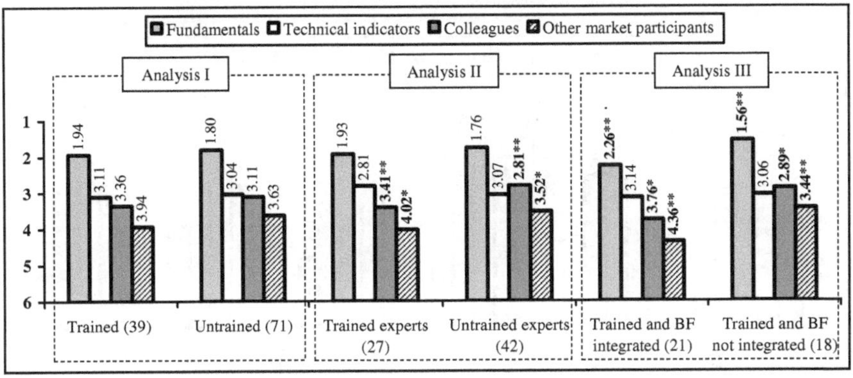

Statements	*All fund managers (mean and number of responses)*	H_0: No difference [(b)]		
		Analysis I	Analysis II	Analysis III
Fundamental facts	*1.82* *115*	-0.686 (0.493)	-0.663 (0.507)	**-2.146**** **(0.032)**
Technical indicators	*3.02* *114*	-0.193 (0.847)	-0.909 (0.363)	-0.365 (0.715)
Colleagues	*3.17* *115*	-1.058 (0.290)	**-1.957*** **(0.050)**	**-1.853*** **(0.064)**
Other market participants	*3.73* *115*	-1.229 (0.219)	**-1.683*** **(0.092)**	**-2.485**** **(0.013)**

(a) The diagram gives the mean answers of the respective group (with the number of responses in parentheses). The importance of each source of information can be assessed by six answering categories, shown on the y-axis, ranging from "highest relevance" (coded as 1) to "no relevance" (coded as 6).

(b) H_0 states that there is no difference between the respective comparison groups. The figures given are the z-value of the Mann-Whitney U-test and the p-value in parentheses.

Stars refer to level of significance: * 10%, ** 5%, *** 1%

Table 3.8: Assessment of investment strategies [(a)] *[STRAT]*

[STRAT] Question: "How intensively do you use the various strategies?
Please allocate 100%."

__% Momentum strategy" __% Contrarian strategy (Value strategy)"
__% Buy-and-Hold strategy" __% Others"

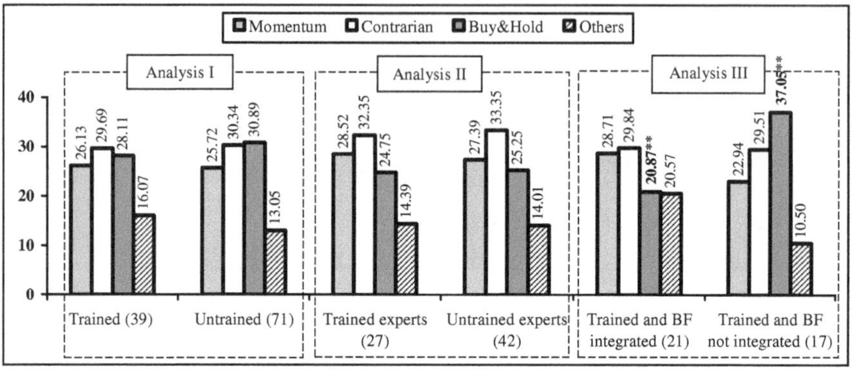

Statements	*All fund managers (mean and number of responses)*	H_0: No difference [(b)]		
		Analysis I	Analysis II	Analysis III
Momentum	*26.27* *108*	-0.293 (0.769)	-0.370 (0.712)	-1.365 (0.172)
Contrarian	*29.31* *108*	-0.069 (0.945)	-0.007 (0.995)	-0.148 (0.882)
Buy-and-Hold	*30.73* *108*	-0.565 (0.572)	-0.488 (0.626)	**-2.095**** **(0.036)**
Others	*13.69* *108*	-0.490 (0.624)	-1.101 (0.920)	-0.934 (0.350)

(a) The diagram gives the mean answers of the respective groups (with the number of responses in parentheses) in %.
(b) H_0 states that there is no difference between the respective comparison groups. The figures given are the z-value of the Mann-Whitney U-test and the p-value in parentheses.
Stars refer to level of significance: * 10%, ** 5%, *** 1%

The results of analysis III in Table 3.8 reveal one further central finding: A significant difference in the ranking of investment strategies between the comparison groups. Trained fund managers in companies where BF is not integrated into investment process rely significantly more on the fundamental buy-and-hold strategy (mean of 37.05%), whereas their comparison group "Trained and BF integrated" shows a clearly lower use of the buy-and-hold (20.87%) but a remarkably higher use of the momentum strategy (28.71%) and other[37] strategies (20.57%). Regarding analyses I and II, it seems that training alone does not noticeably affect the use of investment strategies.[25]

In sum, based on the results presented in Table 3.7 and 3.8, we might conclude that it is rather the integration of BF than training in BF that significantly affects fund managers' investment behavior. In analyses III in Tables 3.7 and 3.8, we find that the group "Trained and BF integrated" significantly differs from its comparison group in its choice of information sources and investment strategies: The group "Trained and BF integrated" relies significantly less strongly on fundamental information and the fundamentally orientated buy-and-hold strategy, but instead more strongly on the behavioral-finance-motivated momentum strategy and other strategies (which are highly probably also based on BF approaches). This orientation seems to point to the expected direction of the analysis: Fund managers in the "Trained and BF integrated" cluster comparatively more strongly aim at benefiting from other market participants' behavioral biases.

3.6 Conclusion

This paper examines the influence of training in BF on professional fund managers' perception and behavior. It is based on a questionnaire survey including answers from more than 100 German fund managers. By separating this sample into "trained" and "untrained" fund managers, i.e. depending on whether they are trained in BF issues or not, we test these groups' perception of markets, their self-assessment as well as their choice of information sources and investment strategies for differences. Additionally, the influence of training only on the group of "experts" in BF is regarded. Furthermore, the effect of integrating BF approaches into investment processes is also analyzed.

37 The answering category "other strategies" is not specified in the questionnaire. In this survey it includes all other strategies being different to the strategies momentum, contrarian, and buy-and-hold.

Results of this study show that training rather influences fund managers' perception than their investment behavior. Training significantly sharpens the awareness towards the reflection effect, which is an important and desirable result, as this bias partly explains the well known disposition effect. Training also remarkably improves the perception of the home bias in the behavior of other fund managers. Furthermore, training reduces the affinity to conformity, which is reflected in a weaker consideration of colleagues and other market participants as information sources. To significantly affect fund managers' investment behavior, the integration of BF approaches in the investment process is needed: Trained fund managers in companies which implement BF in their investment processes assign less importance to fundamental facts, colleagues and other market participants as information sources. Furthermore, they use the fundamental buy-and-hold strategy remarkably less intensively, thereby applying more momentum and other (probably also BF motivated) strategies. This investment behavior indicates a relatively stronger intention to profit from BF biases in the market.

4. Fund managers' information processing in the developed West and the emerging Eastern Europe[38]

4.1 Introduction

Sound information processing is the basis for intelligent decision-making within fiduciary asset management. This global business has spread from developed financial centers to emerging and transition[39] markets. The latter are typically characterized by underdeveloped institutional and regulatory settings, low market efficiency and transparency. Such differing investment environments compared to developed markets are likely to leave their mark on fund managers' investment practices, even though basic investment theories are the same worldwide. Knowledge about fund managers' information processing in markets at different development stages would improve our understanding of their investment behavior, which in turn influences market prices by trades with large volumes of assets.

In this context, Bikhchandani and Sharma (2001) argue that information transparency basically determines the way of information processing and information aggregation in the market: In less developed and less transparent markets information is likely to be revealed and priced more slowly, so that price trends and behavior similar to herding[40] are likely to occur. Accordingly, herding in opaque markets could be efficient if it were part of a price discovery process, i.e. market participants' gradual adjustment to slowly revealed changes

---

38 Helpful comments by Lukas Menkhoff and Torben Lütje are gratefully acknowledged. Furthermore, I would like to thank the surveyed fund managers in the USA, Germany, Russia, and Ukraine for their time offered to respond to the questionnaire as well as their valuable comments provided in our pre-survey interviews. Moreover, my thanks go to the Russian National League of Asset Managers "NLU", the Ukrainian Association of Investment Business "UAIB", and the German Investment Association "BVI" for their relevant recommendation letters and organizational support. Finally, assistance by Ekaterina Gracheva and Torben Lütje in collecting the survey data is gratefully acknowledged.

39 Transition markets are those economies transforming from a central planning system to a market system. They can be regarded as a specific subgroup of emerging markets.

40 Herd behavior or herding is a prominent behavioral finance phenomenon, meaning blindly following trends or the decisions of other market participants, thereby ignoring own private information gained in own research and analysis (for a survey see e.g. Bikhchandani and Sharma, 2001).

in fundamentals. However, it is well known that herding among professional investors is mostly regarded as inefficient in developed markets, as it may drive prices away from their fundamental value or even cause price bubbles (Banerjee, 1992, Bikhchandani et al., 1992, Avery and Zemsky, 1998). These different views on herding do not only suggest that its motivation should be reconsidered in less developed markets, but also indicate potential differences in the use of information in transparent and opaque markets. This paper ties up to these considerations aiming to study fund managers' information processing in markets of different development stages. As representatives for the latter, we consider Western developed markets (DM), i.e. USA and Germany, and Eastern European transition markets (TM), i.e. Russia and Ukraine. Thus, we test the hypothesis that fund managers' information processing differs between DM and TM.

DM and TM provide optimal market settings for our research purpose as they are relatively rich in contrast, especially concerning information availability and thus costs of information acquisition, institutional development, and regulatory restrictions. While DM feature a comparatively high information transparency resulting from stringent (insider trading) disclosure rules and their well-functioning enforcement mechanisms, the investment environment in TM is usually characterized by low transparency. Weak reporting requirements, lower accounting standards, lax enforcement of disclosure laws and regulation, and lack of insider trading prosecution are reasons why TM are seen as less efficient, providing less reliable information on stocks of publicly traded firms. Insofar, our chosen market settings are likely to induce some recognizable effects on fund managers' information processing and investment behavior. This implies that some information categories or behavioral patterns are likely to experience different relevance in DM and TM. It seems particularly likely for TM, that fundamental information might lose its relevance (due to its unavailability or unsoundness) in favor of non-fundamental or private insider information.

Via a questionnaire survey we have collected relevant data on fund managers' perception of markets and themselves as well as the relevance they assign to diverse information categories determining their investment decisions. As such information is not directly observable in markets, surveys provide an appropriate methodology to gain it. Thus, our data is unique in two aspects. First, it provides insights on relevant but difficult-to-access investment professionals. Second, to the best of our knowledge, this is the first academic survey study on fund managers in Eastern European transition markets. It extends related survey-based research on fund managers' views and investment behavior in developed and emerging financial markets (see for example Gehrig et. al. (2009) for the US market; Arnswald (2001), Lütje and Menkhoff (2007) for Continental Europe; Beckmann et al. (2008) for the Asian Emerging Markets).

Our study starts by testing for differences in the business environments in DM and TM, which could possibly influence fund managers' information processing. We find distinctions for the incentive towards short-term performance and relevance of absolute performance for bonus payments, both being significantly higher in TM. Next, we provide comparative evidence from DM and TM on two ways of information processing, i.e. the use of the three basic information categories, which are fundamental facts, technical analysis, and order flow,[41] as well as herd behavior. Here, two core findings are unveiled: Compared to DM, in TM fundamental information loses relevance mostly in favor of order flow. Second striking difference appears in the high level of trend following stated in TM.

In the second part of our study, we follow the argumentation of Bikhchandani and Sharma (2001) by investigating whether the detected TM-features (high relevance assigned to order flow and high level of herding) are possibly price discovery[42] methods. This assumption seems reasonable regarding that in TM publicly available fundamental information is rare or unsound. As proxy for the effort on price discovery, we use fund managers' fundamental orientation. For both DM and TM, we can not identify reliance on order flow to be associated with fundamental orientation, but find support for it to contain rather semi-fundamental information. However, contrary to DM, we do find herd behavior to be positively correlated with fundamental orientation in TM. As such behavior resembles price discovery efforts, it is welcome inasmuch it would promote market efficiency in TM. Besides, when additionally examining motivation for herding in DM and TM, we find that motives documented in the "Western" literature (e.g. career concerns) are crucial for herding in DM, but not (yet) in TM.

Furthermore, we find that a company's size differently influences information processing in DM and TM. In DM, rather small companies tend to both, observing order flow and following trends (herding). By doing so, they seem to deduce information from other (larger, better-informed) market players' actions, probably to compensate for their research constraints. However, in TM, smaller companies do follow trends (though with different motives than in DM),

41 In pre-survey interviews, fund managers named these three information categories as being most important for their decision-making.

42 By price discovery we mean fund managers' analysis to estimate the value of a firm in order to be able to estimate the appropriate market price for this firm.

but they pay less attention to order flow. One rationale for this finding could be that bigger companies probably have a privileged access to order flow in less transparent and less liquid markets. This would also support our results that order flow does not seem to contain fundamental but rather semi-fundamental information (such as planned orders of large own customers or other big traders' trading objectives), which may influence prices only during a day (see e.g. Ito et al., 1998, Gehrig and Menkhoff, 2004).

Returning to our hypothesis, we find supportive evidence for different information processing in DM and TM. As fund managers typically manage huge volumes of assets, their investment decisions are likely to influence market prices – especially in less liquid markets. In turn, fund managers' investment decisions result from their information processing. Hence, our insights into the latter, being new for Russia and Ukraine, contribute to a better understanding of price movements in both DM and TM.

The remainder of the paper contains six sections. Section 4.2 describes our survey data. Section 4.3 addresses information transparency in TM. Section 4.4 aims to identify differences in the business environment of DM and TM, which may influence fund managers' information processing. Section 4.5 presents comparative evidence on the use of three basic information categories and herd behavior in DM and TM. Section 4.6 investigates whether revealed TM-distinctions, i.e. pronounced reliance on order flow and herd behavior, contribute to fund managers' price discovery in TM. Section 4.7 concludes.

4.2 Data

This study is based on a questionnaire survey conducted to gain insights on professional fund managers' behavior and views. As reported in *Table 4.1*, our data pool contains 412 questionnaires from the DM, USA and Germany (received in 2003/2004), as well as 116 questionnaires from the TM, Russia and Ukraine (received in 2007/2008). The difference in the number of questionnaires received from DM and TM is in accordance with their respective markets' size.

In each market, we sent our survey questionnaires to major investment companies, ranked by assets under management. Letters of recommendation provided by the national investment associations in Germany, Russia, and Ukraine supported high participation rates there, ranging between 56% - 77% concerning participating fund management companies.

Table 4.1: The survey sample

	Developed markets		*Transition markets*	
	USA	**Germany**	**Russia**	**Ukraine**
Number of questionnaires	149	263	86	30
Number of participating firms	74	51	58	27
Firm participation rate	29.6%	77.3%	55.7%	65.9%

In detail, though the response rate of 29.6% in the USA could not repeat the success of other markets, the absolute number of participating US firms of 74 is highest compared to other three samples. In Germany, 51 out of 66 addressed member firms of the German Investment Management Association "BVI" participated in our survey, resulting in a firm participation rate of 77.3%. In Russia, in cooperation with the Russian National League of Asset Managers "NLU", we received responses from 58 of 104 contacted companies – a firm participation rate of 55.7%. In Ukraine, again, the helpful support of the Ukrainian Association of Investment Business "UAIB" contributed to participation of 27 out of 41 addressed investment companies – a response rate of 65.9%.[43]

Before starting our survey, we held interviews with fund managers in several financial centers in the USA and Germany, as well as in Moscow, and Kiev. These pre-survey interviews served to ensure that questionnaire contents and response categories are formulated in an appropriate and accepted manner. In particular, for enabling reliable cross-country comparisons, the wording in the respective survey languages, i.e. English, German and Russian, is assured to be correct, well understood and express the same issue. Moreover, guaranteed anonymity to all participants as well as the offer to provide them with survey results gives low incentives for strategic answering.[44]

43 In contrast to Russia, the Ukrainian fund industry is dominated by venture capital funds, which absolute number accounted for 410 of existent 519 funds in 2006. We possess additional 26 questionnaires from fund managers of venture capital funds. However, within this cross-country study, we only consider answers from 30 fund managers of non-venture-capital funds, managing mutual and pension funds.

44 Bonus payments are generally considered as a confidential compensation detail. However, over 70% of our surveyed fund managers have indicated the size of their bonus. This fact certainly confirms their trust in anonymous and confidential treatment of their answers (which we pointed out in every questionnaire) and thus their open-minded attitude towards the whole survey.

For our research purpose, we compare the survey results from the USA and Germany on the one hand to those from Russia and Ukraine on the other hand, intending to highlight specific differences between DM and TM. Additionally, also the comparison of both TM appears interesting, as their market share of open-end mutual funds (where fund units can be bought and sold at any time) remarkably differs.[45]

4.3 On information transparency and efficiency in Russia and Ukraine

General relevance of markets' information transparency is highlighted by classic theoretical works like e.g. Diamond (1985): Releasing information of publicly traded firms leads to welfare improvements. This implicates that higher information disclosure quality reduces investors' needs to collect costly (unpublished) private information, thus saving their effort on this action.

However, information disclosure quality in Russia and Ukraine – meaning the precision, timeliness, and quantity of provided information to investors – is still insufficient. Reporting requirements and accounting standards are relatively weak, not fully fulfilled even by large enterprises. Thus, for our research purpose, these two TM are particularly suitable as representatives for markets with low information transparency and efficiency. This section reviews studies confirming this.

EBRD[46]-studies on securities markets in transition economies find that, though stock markets' legislation is Russia and Ukraine is mostly in good compliance with international principles, good laws alone are not enough to establish efficient markets. Both, the quality of regulation and the effectiveness its enforcement mechanisms, need to be improved in order to strengthen investors' trust in financial markets. So far, e.g. firms' prospectuses[47] often omit risk-sensitive information. Furthermore, their reliability may generally be cast

45 The share of open-end funds is 1.7% in Ukraine, but 47.6% in Russia. The remaining shares consist of closed-end funds (diversified or not diversified) as well as "interval" funds, units of which can be bought or sold only during determined time intervals. This data is provided by the Ukrainian investment association UAIB.

46 European Bank for Reconstruction and Development (EBRD)

47 The prospectus is a formal legal document that provides details about an investment offered for sale to the public. It contains a company's facts an investor needs to know in order to make an informed investment decision, i.e. degree of disclosure, risk identification, quality of financial reporting, institutional oversight, and distribution practices of the company.

into doubt due to the mild sanctions for providing inaccurate or misleading information. In Russia, regulation still underlies some political pressure and rarely exercises its authority, though possessing an effective supervising capacity (see e.g. Cigna and Chapaev, 2008).

Studies based on surveys and interviews conducted among Russian accountants and international auditors also reveal the consensus that Russian financial statements do not properly reflect a company's economic status quo as well as that corporate governance standards in Russia are de facto still very weak. Large international enterprises publish their quarterly reports with a huge delay, sometimes exceeding one year (Rozhnova, 2000, Preobragenskaya and McGee, 2003a, 2004). One Russian oil producing company did not present its annual report for 2003 for more than two years, even despite its NYSE listing (Kochetygova et al., 2005). In sum, the disclosure of information being relevant for investors – e.g. early releases of IFRS/US GAAP financials, terms of employment contracts with CEOs, details of directors' and executives' remuneration – remains very low (Stepanov et al, 2009).[48] Furthermore, there are weak regulation enforcements on insider trading in Russia. Studies found strong evidence for private information trading in the Russian stock market, taking place especially around major corporate events and being predictive about firms' future economic performance (Christoffersen and Slok, 2000, Grishchenko et al., 2002, Wölfle, 2009). Due to undisclosed insider trading, superior information of insiders and local investors is likely to be incorporated in stock prices through their trades.[49]

In Ukraine, trading of securities at the unregulated over-the-counter (OTC) market – where brokers, dealers and investors usually trade over the phone or computer and do not reveal their trading information to other market participants – is much higher than trading at regulated information providing places (such as the leading organized trading place PFTS). Since 1998, OTC trading usually exceeded 85% of total securities trading in the country. The only information that the OTC market reports to the SSMSC[50], the major regulatory body of the stock market in Ukraine, are the volumes of securities traded there. Thus, lack of

48 The study also shows that listing abroad and the requirements of foreign regulators are important to improve the informational transparency of a company.

49 When analyzing the fund management industry in TM, it should be kept in mind that there is a high concentration and low liquidity of most stocks, relative lack of transparency in mutual funds' operations as well as no high-quality rating systems of individual mutual funds. E.g. in Russia, 90% of market capitalization is concentrated on 16 Russian corporations.

50 Securities and Stock Market State Commission

information on the OTC trading strongly hinders research on Ukrainian stock market.

Regarding such lack of transparency in TM compared to the sound reporting standards and their enforcement in DM, it seems reasonable to expect that information procurement and processing might vary in DM and TM. In particular, for valuation of securities, fundamental facts might lose their relevance (due to their unavailability or unsoundness) in favor of non-fundamental or private insider information.

4.4 Evidence on market settings in DM and TM

4.4.1 Motivation

For better understanding of our results on information processing in Section 4.5, we first aim to gain an impression on the market settings in DM and TM. Differences in fund managers' perceived level of information, their view on market efficiency, given performance incentives, and chosen research effort might also influence their choice of processed information.

Thinking of research on information asymmetry resulting in local information advantages in emerging markets (e.g. Dvorak, 2005, and Chang, 2009)[51], it is interesting to question whether our respondents' in DM and TM belief to possess *information advantages on domestic securities*, particularly compared to foreign investors. Statement [1] in *Table 4.2* aims to gain insights on this.

The choice of information is usually consistent with a fund manager's *view on the efficiency of markets* he operates in (see e.g. Menkhoff and Nikiforow, 2009). The stronger fund managers perceive market biases, the less they regard their markets as fully efficient. This could increase the motivation to use non-fundamental information, e.g. in order to profitably exploit market

51 Literature on information processing in less developed and less transparent investment environments includes a strand of empirical studies analyzing the effects of information asymmetries on investors' performance. Focusing mostly on Asian emerging equity markets, the question is whether domestic investors possess local information advantages, which allow them to perform better than more sophisticated foreign investors (e.g. Choe et al., 2001, Seasholes, 2004). In this respect, Dvorak (2005) and Chang (2009) provide a relevant finding: Even though domestic investors' do possess short-lived information advantages, in the long run it is the combination of both, domestic investors' local information and foreign investors' (e.g. global brokerages) investment expertise, which leads to superior performance.

inefficiencies. By the degree fund managers agree to statement [2] on the belief in the predominant influence of psychology on market prices (rather than fundamentals), and to statements [3] on the perception of selective/biased information processing in the market[52], we are able to reveal and compare the degree of perceived market inefficiencies in DM and TM.

In addition, fund managers' investment behavior including their choice of information may be affected by their *incentives* – set on the part of their clients and company. For example, a higher demand for short-term profits, e.g. on the part of fund managers' clients, might lead to a comparatively higher reliance on non-fundamental information. By contrast, a long-term performance orientation would rather require investments based on fundamental analysis. An investment strategy aiming at generating short-term returns (e.g. momentum strategy) is generally associated with high trading activity, contrary to long-term orientated strategies (e.g. buy-and-hold or value investment strategies). Thus, we formulate the statement [4] to learn about fund managers *incentives towards short-term performance*. It should be kept in mind that even though short-term performance orientation may be desirable from the clients' point of view, it is rather a "misleading" incentive (at least in DM) as studies found excessive short-term trading activity to be performance-hurting (e.g. Odean, 1999).

Investment companies aim to influence the behavior of their fund managers by rewarding them with bonus payments for "good performance". Therefore, we are interested in revealing whether "good performance" is defined the same in DM and TM. Regarding *bonus criteria as incentives*, some literature suggests that relevance of relative performance for bonus payments may lead to inefficient outcomes in the market as fund managers are likely to invest not enough effort in getting (particularly fundamental) information (e.g. Eichberger et al., 1999). However, contrary evidence is provided by Gehrig et al. (2009), finding bonus payments and relative performance as bonus criterion to be positively related to higher working effort and stronger fundamental orientation.[53] We are able to tests for differences between DM and TM regarding the relevance for three bonus criteria, i.e. absolute (issue [5]) and relative fund performance ([6]) as well as subjective assessment by superiors and colleagues ([7]).

52 Disregarding information if it does not confirm one's own opinion describes the "confirmation bias" – psychologically motivated, selective information processing, which is well-documented in the behavioral finance and psychology literature (Festinger, 1957, Nickerson, 1998, Pronin, 2007).

53 Gehrig et al. (2009) rely on the same survey data for the USA and Germany as we do. In their study, they compare the US market and the Central European markets Germany and Switzerland.

Table 4.2: Evidence on fund mangers' market perception and market settings related to information processing (1)

Please assess the following statements
(six answering categories ranging from "completely agree" (coded as 1) to "complete disagree" (6))

[1] As a domestic asset manager I benefit from better information on domestic securities compared to market players overseas.

[2] People are not machines; thus security prices are clearly more determined by psychological influences than by fundamentals.

[3] Asset managers often disregard some information if it does not complement their opinion.

[4] I often trade too much, as my clients demand short-term performance.

If you receive a performance-based remuneration, which criteria determine the size of that bonus?
(six answering categories ranging from "highest relevance" (coded as 1) to "no relevance" (6))

[5] Absolute fund performance **[6]** Relative fund performance **[7]** Subjective assessment by superiors/colleagues

[8] Average period of data procurement and research (in hours per week)

Panel A:	Share of agreement in % and Mean 1)					**Panel B:** DM vs. TM		
	Developed Markets		*Transition Markets*		H_0: (2) No difference RUS and UA	Mean 1)		H_0: (2) No difference DM and TM
	USA	**GER**	**RUS**	**UA**		**DM**	**TM**	
[1] Perception of domestic information advantage	71.5% 3.0	65.2% 3.2	59.5% 3.2	80.0% 2.6	**-2.135**** **(0.033)**	3.2	3.1	-0.902 (0.367)
[2] Market view: Psychology dominates fundamentals	63.6% 3.2	77.4% 2.8	75.9% 2.7	66.7% 3.0	-1.243 (0.214)	2.9	2.8	-1.215 (0.224)
[3] Market view: Confirmation bias	87.9% 2.4	58.0% 3.3	63.2% 3.1	58.6% 3.3	-0.973 (0.330)	3.0	3.2	-1.489 (0.136)
[4] Incentive: Short-term performance	14.3% 4.9	17.2% 4.8	24.7% 4.4	23.3% 4.3	-0.761 (0.446)	4.8	4.4	**-2.965***** **(0.003)**
[5] Incentive: Absolute performance	35.9% 4.3	34.1% 4.1	73.4% 2.4	73.7% 3.1	-1.448 (0.147)	4.2	2.5	**-8.050***** **(0.000)**
[6] Incentive: Relative performance	80.4% 2.4	80.0% 2.5	81.3% 2.4	64.7% 3.2	**1.837*** **(0.066)**	2.4	2.6	-1.117 (0.264)
[7] Incentive: Assessment by superiors	74.2% 2.8	85.9% 2.4	46.0% 3.8	56.3% 3.2	-1.535 (0.125)	2.6	3.7	**-6.850***** **(0.000)**
[8] Effort on information research	21.0 hours	20.1 hours	20.7 hours	19.0 hours	-0.473 (0.637)	20.5	20.3	-0.592 (0.553)

(1) For statements 1-7, according to the encodings, a mean of 3.5 or less indicates rather agreement with the statement. Panel A: The share of agreement is calculated as the sum of answers given to answering categories 1-3. The mean refers to all six categories. Panel B: The means for the developed (DM) and transition markets (TM) are calculated after pooling the answers from USA and Germany and those from Russia and Ukraine, respectively.

(2) The figures given are the *z*-value of the Mann–Whitney *U*-test with *p*-value in parentheses.

Stars refer to level of significance: * 10%, ** 5%, *** 1%

Finally, fund managers' information procurement and processing may also depend on the effort they are willing to invest in information research. One might expect that collecting and interpreting non-fundamental information (e.g. observing the order flow or following trends) is less time-consuming and less sophisticated than analyzing fundamental information (e.g. evaluating financial statements or assessing future development of companies and markets). Thus, a lower *research effort* might result in a higher preference for non-fundamental information. On the other hand, procurement of non-fundamental information might be costly and time-consuming, too, if it implicates e.g. deducing unpublished relevant information from private information sources as part of a price discovery process. Whether the effort on data procurement and research varies between DM and TM can be answered by issue [8].

Before coming to results, there is one further aspect we should keep in mind. The population in TM is yet rather mistrustful towards modern investment products, like e.g. mutual funds. In personal interviews prior to our survey, Russian and Ukrainian fund managers strongly emphasized their current effort on informing the population about the advantages of investing in funds (instead of keeping money on bank deposits or even at home). Is this specific of TM recognizable in our comparative analysis?

4.4.2 Results

The results in Tables 4.2 are presented as follows. Each of the statement can be assessed by six answering categories, ranging from "completely agree" or "highest relevance" (coded as 1) to "completely disagree" or "no relevance" (coded as 6). Panel A reports the shares of agreement to the respective statements (calculated as the sum of answering categories 1-3) and the means (of all six categories) for all four markets USA, Germany, Russia, and Ukraine, separately. In the last column of Panel A, the Mann-Whitney U-test (MWU-test) indicates whether the mean answers of Russian and Ukrainian fund managers significantly differ. Panel B gives the results of the MWU-test on differences between DM and TM. The means for DM and TM are calculated after pooling the answers from USA and Germany to the sample of DM and those from Russia and Ukraine to the sample of TM.

The results of the MWU-test in Panel B indeed unveil some significant differences between market settings in DM and TM.

For statement [4], the respective shares of agreement in Panel A indicate that the majority of respondents in each country disagree about trading too much as their clients demand *short-term performance* – which ought to be good news in general. However, fund managers in TM agree to this statement comparatively more strongly than do their peers in DM (Panel B: DM-mean of 4.8 versus a TM-mean of 4.4). This result signalizes a comparatively higher short-term orientation and trading activity in TM, which may reduce the relevance of fundamental information in TM compared to DM.

Besides, significant differences also appear regarding *bonus criteria.* Interestingly, even though the size of bonus payments seems not to depend on the development stage of a financial market,[54] the relevance of bonus-determining criteria significantly does. While the bonus criterion "relative" fund performance [item 6] is of almost equal relevance in both, DM and TM (means of 2.4 and 2.6)[55], the importance of "absolute" fund performance enjoys highest relevance in TM (2.5), but gets least relevant in DM (4.2). In contrast, the "assessment by superiors and colleagues" is highly important for fund managers in DM (2.6), while their peers in TM regard this criterion as least important (3.7).

Apparently, these results seem to identify different competitors whom fund managers face in DM and TM. One possible interpretation for our results might be the following: To be successful in a highly competitive environment of DM, a fund manager has to set himself apart from his peers. These are other fund managers in the market, competing with whom is relevant to gain clients (relative performance), as well as colleagues within the own company, competing with whom by e.g. soft skills may be relevant for a promotion within the company (assessment by superiors and colleagues). In contrast, fund managers in TM are opposed to many potential clients. The latter are, however, mistrustful towards new investment products and prefer keeping their money at home or on bank deposits, as already mentioned above. To increase the demand for fund investments, i.e. to attract the interest and capital of the population, it seems to require achieving high absolute returns (absolute performance) to probably beat the returns of other financial products such as bank deposits. This would be in line with the information we received in our pre-survey interviews.

Apart from this, the remaining factors on information processing do not significantly differ between DM and TM. Fund managers in all four markets do

---

54 In our survey sample, the average size of the bonus Russian fund managers receive additionally to their fixed salary is 65% (n=67). This is more than twice as high as indicated by German respondents (30%, n=173) and even 3.5 times as high as stated by Ukrainian fund managers (18%, n=21). However, comparatively outstanding is the average bonus of 183% in the USA (n=122).

55 The remarkably low relevance for relative performance in Ukraine may be attributable to the absence of an accepted benchmark in the market, as noticed by Ukrainian fund managers in personal interviews.

not regard their business environment as fully efficient, as each market sample rather agrees to statements [1]–[3] (indicated by shares of agreement above 58% as well as sample means below 3.5).[56] Results for item [8] report that also the effort on data procurement and research is quite similar in DM and TM, ranging from 19 hours in Ukraine to 21 hours in the USA.

Interestingly, compared to Russia and also to both DM, Ukrainian fund managers outstandingly strongly (mean of 2.6) perceive to be better informed on domestic securities than foreign investors ([1]) and assign lowest (mean of 3.2) relevance to relative fund performance as bonus criterion ([6]). In our pre-survey interviews fund managers mentioned that an accepted benchmark was not yet fully established in the Ukrainian market. This hint could at least partly explain our latter result.

In summary, fund managers' view on market efficiency would justify a certain use of non-fundamental information in both DM and TM. However, we reveal fund managers in DM and TM to face different performance incentives. This could predict a relatively higher reliance on non-fundamental information in TM, as evidence suggests that the incentive for achieving high absolute returns in a short period of time (through high trading activity) is significantly higher in TM than in DM.

4.5 Evidence on information processing in DM and TM

4.5.1 Hypotheses for the use of basic information categories

In our pre-survey interviews, fund managers named "fundamentals" (economic and political hard facts), "technical analysis" (charts and quantitative indicators) and "order flow" (observed transactions) as most important information categories for investment decision-making.

The analysis of fundamental facts – i.e. underlying macroeconomic factors as well as company-specific factors that influence a security's value (a

56 In all four markets, we find that fund managers' attitude towards market efficiency consistently determines their market perception. The more they agree on the superior influence of psychology (rather than fundamentals) on prices [2], the more they are aware of market inefficiencies "confirmation bias" [3] and "herding" (which will be discussed later in Section 4.5.3). This significant result is revealed by correlating the respective answers.

company's actual business and its future prospects) – aims at measuring the intrinsic value of a security. It is a comparatively extensive and time-consuming analysis, which is often regarded as the cornerstone of investing. Technical analysis does not attempt to measure a security's intrinsic value. Instead, it regards only the history of prices in order to identify past price patterns, which are then used to derive future price developments. Finally, also information gained from observing the order flow might forecast price movements. Considering flows can either be regarded as rational learning from other participants' fundamental analysis (Kyle, 1985) or as analysis of semi-fundamental information (about e.g. presently executed or planned orders of other traders), which may have impact on prices only in the short-term, but not in the medium-term (see e.g. Ito et al., 1998; Covrig and Melvin, 2002).[57]

From literature we know that investment professionals use these three information categories independently from each other as they are relevant for different time horizons (e.g. Arnswald, 2001, Gehrig and Menkhoff, 2004). However, the relevance of these three information categories may differ between DM and TM due to their differing investment environments. Evidence in Section 4.3 outlines lack of sound and regularly published corporate fundamental information and existence of insider trading in TM. In Section 4.4 it appears that fund managers in TM have comparatively higher incentive towards short-term performance. Combining this evidence, two aspects seem to distinct fund managers in TM from their peers in DM: First, they act in rather opaque investment environments; second, their pressure to succeed in shorter time horizons is comparatively higher.

Fund managers rely on that information which helps them best in achieving their investment goals. Hence, we may hypothesize non-fundamental (or exclusive insider) information sources to gain relevance in TM compared to DM. Observing order flow and price trends may be informative as both are likely to contain private or insider information of better informed traders. This is particularly likely when market's transparency is low and information asymmetry high. The use of non-fundamental information in TM could thus compensate for the lack or unsoundness of available fundamental information.

Accordingly, we test two basic hypotheses:

57 A comprehensive study of possible views on and justifications for flow analysis is provided by Gehrig and Menkhoff (2004).

Hypothesis 1: *Fund managers' information processing differs between DM and TM.*

Hypothesis 2: *Compared to fund managers in DM, fund mangers in TM more strongly rely on non-fundamental information.*

Is this really the case?

4.5.2 Evidence on the use of basic information categories

To shed more light on fund managers' information processing, we aim to learn about their relative importance assigned to fundamental facts, technical analysis and order flow when making investment decisions. *Figure 4.1.A* shows the received answers.

Our results clearly confirm the expectations formulated in both hypotheses. Even though the ranking of the three information categories is identical, the relative importance attached to each single information category significantly differs between DM and TM.[58]

In all four markets "fundamental facts" are assigned a major role for investment decision-making (more than 50% in each country), followed by non-fundamental information categories "technical analysis" and "order flows", both representing a kind of complementary information. However, fundamental information experiences higher relevance in DM than in TM, particularly in the USA (77.9%). Regarding non-fundamental information, there is no clear pattern for the use of technical analysis, but an astonishingly clear one for the use of order flow. Being least relevant in DM, order flow significantly gains relevance in TM: Compared to 5.9% in the USA and 9.6% in Germany, these are 15.9% in Russia and even 22.5% in Ukraine.

Additionally, our surveyed fund managers are asked to indicate their personal forecasting horizon when using the three information categories. The results shown in *Figure 4.1.B* support the literature, showing that in both, DM and TM, the analysis of fundamental information enables rather long-term forecasts (months to years); technical analysis contains information for medium-term price movements (mostly weeks), whereas order flow is mostly considered in the short run (intraday to days).[59]

58 According to the MWU-test, the differences between the DM- and TM-means are significant at 1% level (not given in the Figure).

59 For the profitability of technical analysis and the use of order flow see e.g. Grinblatt et al. (1995), Jegadeesh and Titman (2001), Keim and Madhavan (1995), Gehrig and Menkhoff (2004), Menkhoff and Schmidt (2005).

Figure 4.1: Evidence on the use of three basic information categories

[A] How much importance do you attach to the following categories of information? Please assign 100% altogether.

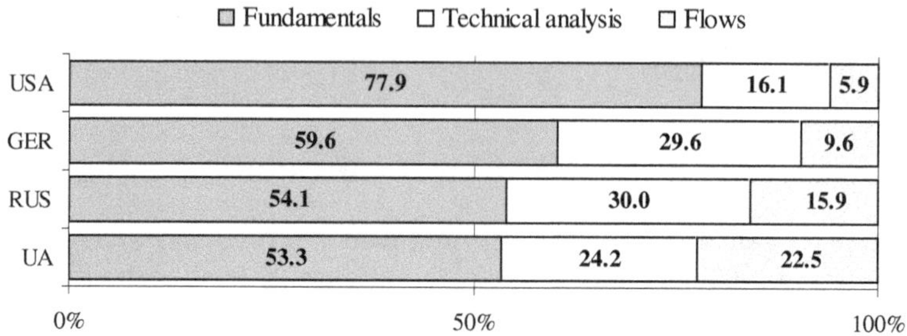

[B] What is your personal forecasting horizon when using this information?

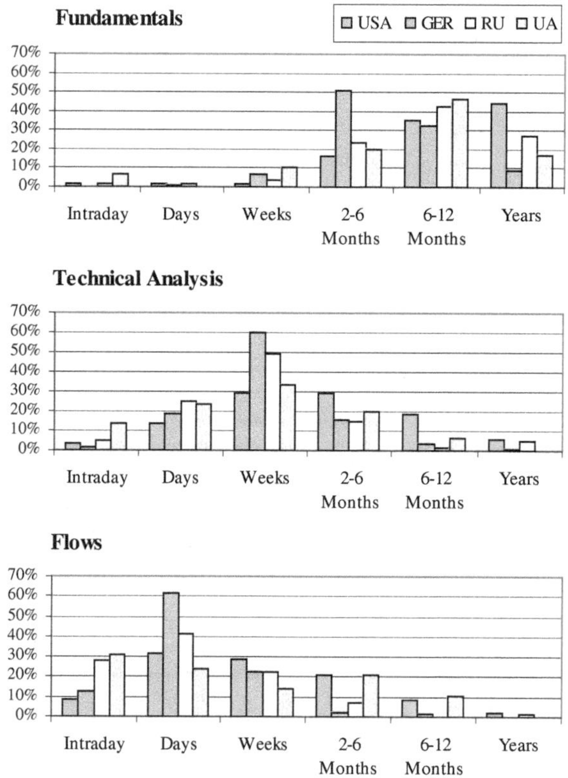

A remarkable difference between DM and TM appears again for the order flow: Whereas only 10% of fund managers in DM assess order flow as relevant for their intraday forecasts, these are up to 30% in TM. Thus, in TM, relatively more information processing seems to take place in the very short-run, i.e. during a day. Such attention to order flow may indicate its profitability (exploiting short-term price movements) or market's higher uncertainty regarding true values of investments.

So far, our results confirm both Hypotheses, 1 and 2. Particularly, the relevance assigned to order flow turns out to be the key distinction between DM and TM.

4.5.3 Evidence on herding

Herding describes the tendency to (blindly) follow other market participants (or just trends), thereby often ignoring own private information, gained from own research. Bikhchandani and Sharma (2001) have noted that in opaque investment environments (of emerging markets) information is likely to be revealed and priced more slowly, thus causing price trends. Consequently, herd behavior might result from investors' price discovery process, i.e. their gradual adjustment to new, but slowly revealed fundamental information. However, besides this efficient type of herding, Bikhchandani and Sharma also mention the high probability of reputational herding and information cascades in emerging markets. Following this plausible thoughts, we dedicate a separate analysis of herd behavior in our sample, as it can be a relevant part of fund managers' information processing.

Our survey included statements to grasp both, fund managers' perception of herding in the market as well as their degree to herd themselves. According to *Table 4.3*, fund managers in DM perceive herding among other fund managers (statement [1]) to a striking high degree (shares of agreement of 91%, DM-mean of 2.3). This is significantly higher compared to our respondents in TM (TM-mean of 3.0). Statement [2] "I generally follow the trend" serves to detect fund managers' tendency to herd themselves. In that case, fund mangers in TM indicate to be trend followers to a significantly higher degree (TM-mean of 2.9) than their peers in DM (DM-mean of 3.9). Especially astonishing is the degree of trend following in Russia, which is highest in the whole sample with a mean of 2.8 and a share of agreement of 76%.

Table 4.3: Evidence on herd behavior [1)]

Please assess the following statements (six answering categories ranging from "completely agree" (coded as 1) to "complete disagree" (6))

[1] Herding is observable amongst professional fund managers.

[2] I generally follow the trend.

Panel A:	Share of agreement in % and Mean [(1)]					**Panel B:** DM vs. TM		
	Developed Markets		*Transition Markets*		H_0: [(2)] No difference RUS and UA	Mean [1)]		H_0: [(2)] No difference DM and TM
	USA	**GER**	**RUS**	**UA**		**DM**	**TM**	
[1] Perception of herding in the market	90.5% 2.2	91.2% 2.3	73.6% 2.9	70.0% 3.2	-0.906 (0.365)	2.3	3.0	**-6.402***** **(0.000)**
[2] Own herd behavior	21.0% 4.4	50.2% 3.7	75.6% 2.8	66.5% 3.2	**-1.943**** **(0.052)**	3.9	2.9	**-7.480***** **(0.000)**

(1) Panel A: The share of agreement is calculated as the sum of answers given to answering categories 1-3. The mean refers to all six categories. Panel B: The means for the developed (DM) and transition markets (TM) are calculated after pooling the answers from USA and Germany and those from Russia and Ukraine, respectively. According to the encodings, a mean of 3.5 or less indicates rather agreement with the statement.

(2) The figures given are the *z*-value of the Mann–Whitney *U*-test with *p*-value in parentheses.

Stars refer to level of significance: * 10%, ** 5%, *** 1%

Next relevant finding appears when comparing the answers to both statements with each other: Fund managers in USA and Germany observe herding in the behavior of others to a much higher degree (means of 2.2 and 2.3 respectively) than they admit to follow the trend themselves (4.4 and 3.7). In contrast, such a discrepancy between the market view and self-perception does not exist in our Eastern European sample of TM. Here, the answers to both statements are almost the same (means of 2.9 and. 2.8 in Russia; 3.2 and 3.2 in Ukraine).

Summing up, also this evidence rather supports our hypotheses. The high degree of herding in TM should attract special research attention to examine whether it contributes to market efficiency or rather reduces it. We will shed light on the motives for herding in DM and TM in the following sections.

4.6 Order flow, herding and relevance of fundamental information in DM and TM

According to our core analysis in Section 4.5, there are two key distinctive features in the information processing of fund managers in DM and TM, i.e. the importance assigned to order flow as well as the degree of herd behavior. Both are high in TM.

The high occurrence of order flow and herd behavior in TM may cause concerns regarding their effects on market efficiency. Thus, we question whether these TM-features probably belong to Eastern European fund managers' price discovery methods. This would particularly be the case, if they were simultaneously related to high fundamental orientation. In that case, order flow and herd behavior could not only be justified by the lack of information transparency in TM, but also represent Eastern European fund managers' effort to contribute to their markets' efficiency. To shed light on this, in this section we aim to analyze the motives for flow observation and herd behavior in DM and TM, respectively.

4.6.1 Order flow, herding and company size

We start our analysis by examining whether the reliance on order flow and herd behavior are complementary actions, which would particularly strengthen their role for price discovery in TM.

Interestingly, *Table 4.4* reveals a distinguishing result: Even though the use of order flow and herding are positively correlated in DM, their correlation is significantly negative in TM. This indicates that, contrary to DM, in TM the use of order flow and herd behavior tend to exclude each other. Such occurrence of "types" among fund managers, which are not observable in DM, is likely to reflect some institutional effects.

Generally, the size of the investment company (measured by assets under management) a fund manager is working at is crucial for his choice of information. It determines his given research resources (e.g. number of fund managers in a company and their aggregated working time) and thus the possible extensiveness of his information research and analysis. While big institutions with many fund managers can afford an extensive research, one might assume that information procurement is more costly for small fund management companies with less aggregated working time for research and analysis.

Table 4.4: The use of order flow, herd behavior, and company size

Coefficients of the Spearman Rank Correlation (p-value)	*Developed Markets*		*Transition Markets*	
	USA	**GER**	**RUS**	**UA**
	Importance of order flow			
Herd behavior (1)	0.023 (0.778)	0.097 (0.120)	**-0.189*** **(0.083)**	**-0.399**** **(0.029)**
	Company size (1)			
Importance of order flow	-0.115 (0.172)	-0.097 (0.121)	0.158 (0.154)	0.273 (0.145)
Herd behavior	-0.111 (0.186)	**-0.253***** **(0.000)**	-0.139 (0.211)	**-0.482***** **(0.007)**

(1) "Herd behavior" stands for the statement "I generally follow the trend", as reported in Table 4.3. "Size of the company" means the volume of assets under management. The coefficients are adjusted to simplify interpretation.
Stars refer to level of significance: * 10%, ** 5%, *** 1%

These costs might be even higher in less transparent TM, where small companies are less likely to possess private or insider information compared to bigger companies. Hence, for small firms, it could be reasonable and rational to profit from other (big) players' (fundamental) analysis by simply following their actions. Thus, we assume small companies to possess less accurate private information compared to bigger ones.

Indeed, the correlations with company's size complement the picture (Table 4.4): Whereas herd behavior is practiced rather by smaller companies in both DM and TM, order flow turns out to be relevant for smaller companies in DM, but for bigger ones in TM. The respective correlations are all close to significance.[60] To resolve this "puzzle", we address the respective motives for the use of order flow and herd behavior in the following sections.

60 Nevertheless, our results (not shown in Table 4) confirm the expectation that in both, DM and TM, big companies tend to rely more on the use of fundamental information and less on technical analysis.

4.6.2 Order flow and fundamental orientation

There are different justifications for the use of order flow in the literature. They can be comprehensibly presented by relating them to market players' size. For small companies, it seems reasonable to gain information from the order flow in order to compensate for their research constraints. Hence, according to "actions speak louder than words", small firms might make inferences about the (better informed) big players' private information or learn about their fundamental analysis by observing their trading, i.e. their order flow (Kyle, 1985). On the other hand, if flow analysis rather contains semi-fundamental private information, then it is expected to be most informative for big companies, which have a better access to it (Covrig and Melvin, 2001, Gehrig and Menkhoff, 2004). Semi-fundamental information would be e.g. the knowledge about a big client's order, which is not yet executed, but might have an impact on prices after execution. Also the information about short-term trading objectives of other traders, which might influence only short-term price movements (without being relevant for medium-term prices), can be exploited by flow analysis.

Is the use of order flow fundamentally orientated, particularly in TM? To examine which type of information can be gained from order flow, we aim to find out which "infotype" the users of order flow belong to. Our survey data contains information on the relevance fund managers assign to six further information sources. As reported in *Table 4.5*, we group fundamental facts, discussions with colleagues and statements of economic opinion leaders on the one hand and charts/technical analysis, investment decisions of other market players and statements of opinion leaders of the industry on the other hand.

Fund managers assigning high relevance to the first three information categories can be regarded as fundamentally orientated, as relying on this kind of information signalizes fund managers' willingness to own extensive security analysis, including interpretation of fundamental and economic facts and serious discussions with colleagues. By contrast, those who rely on the latter three information categories rather signalize interest in reducing their own research effort by focusing on comparably less sophisticated chart analysis, following investment decisions (and thus analysis) of other market players or advices of opinion leaders within the asset management industry.

The correlation results in Table 4.5 reveal flow users to be of rather similar type in DM and TM. Common significant characteristics are a lower reliance on fundamental information, but a higher one on investment decisions of other market players. These results also hold in the multivariate TOBIT regression (Table 4.5).

Table 4.5: Use of order flow and other information sources [(1)]

	Developed Markets		*Transition Markets*	
	USA	**GER**	**RUS**	**UA**
Coefficients of the Spearman Rank Correlation (p-value)	Importance of order flow			
Fundamental facts about the company / market	-0.086 (0.300)	**-0.126**** **(0.042)**	**-0.265**** **(0.014)**	**-0.428**** **(0.018)**
Discussions / exchange of views with colleagues	-0.026 (0.757)	0.084 (0.177)	0.116 (0.290)	**0.349*** **(0.059)**
Statements of economic opinion leaders	**0.366***** **(0.000)**	**0.272***** **(0.000)**	0.110 (0.315)	0.296 (0.112)
Chart analysis / technical indicators	0.102 (0.219)	**0.107*** **(0.086)**	-0.028 (0.802)	0.025 (0.894)
Investment decision of other market players	**0.481***** **(0.000)**	**0.433***** **(0.000)**	**0.239**** **(0.027)**	0.112 (0.554)
Statements of opinion leaders within the industry	0.014 (0.867)	**0.297***** **(0.000)**	0.034 (0.759)	0.126 (0.508)
Coefficients of the Censored TOBIT regression (p-value)	Importance of order flow			
Fundamental facts	-0.763 (0.541)	**-1.752**** **(0.040)**	**-4.695***** **(0.001)**	**-8.203***** **(0.003)**
Colleagues	-1.038 (0.285)	0.949 (0.175)	1.850 (0.201)	**5.527**** **(0.017)**
Other market players	**7.020***** **(0.000)**	**4.358***** **(0.000)**	**2.709*** **(0.062)**	-2.088 (0.305)
Constant	**23.123***** **(0.000)**	**24.709***** **(0.000)**	**22.986***** **(0.000)**	13.783 (0.132)
Adjusted R^2	0.218	0.146	0.168	0.229
Number	147	258	85	30

(1) For the assessment of these sources of information used in making investment decisions, there are six answering categories, ranging from "highest relevance" (coded as 1) to "no relevance" (coded as 6). All coefficients are multiplied by (-1) to simplify interpretation.
Stars refer to level of significance: * 10%, ** 5%, *** 1%

In the TOBIT regressions we only include three information categories in order to focus the analysis on its two possible outcomes: Fundamental facts control for the intention to learn about other participants' fundamental analysis; colleagues (who possibly may provide information about the orders of company's own clients) and other market participants (e.g. other traders) account for possible semi-fundamental information in order flow. In all four markets the picture is similar: The more relevance fund managers assign to investment decisions of other market participants (in USA, GER, and RUS) and colleagues (in UA) and the less they rely on fundamentals, the higher is their orientation on order flow.

We conclude that relying on order flow as information source does not seem to display any fundamental orientation, even not in TM. Our analysis rather supports order flow to contain semi-fundamental information. Particularly for TM, this would be in line with high importance assigned to order flow during short time horizons (intraday to days; Figure 4.1.B) and with higher attention paid to order flow by big companies in TM (Table 4.4). The latter can be expected to have a privileged access to semi-fundamental information in their markets, compared to smaller companies.

4.6.3 Herding and fundamental orientation

Evidence on the high degree of herding in TM, documented in Section 4.5.3, should attract special research attention because opportunistic or uniformed herding might reduce market efficiency. In addition, the validity of "Western" motives for herd behavior should be reconsidered in TM. This need arises from the argumentation of Bikhchandani and Sharma (2001) that in less developed markets with low transparency information is likely to be revealed and priced more slowly. Thus, price trends and herding are more likely to occur, but they could be characterized efficient. Hence, there should be a distinctive view on the motivations for herding, depending on whether it takes place in DM or TM.

Research on herding in DM (see Bikhchandani and Sharma, 2001) basically differentiates between the efficient "spurious" herding which is fundamentals-driven, i.e. when investors react to commonly known public information (investors are not reversing their decision after observing others) and the "intentional" herding. The latter is not efficient if it results from the intention to copy the behavior of other investors, thereby ignoring own private information. However, intentional herd behavior in financial markets can be rational if it is due to concerns for reputation, compensation schemes, or imperfect information.

Herding due to *reputation concerns* (Scharfstein and Stein, 1990, Graham, 1999, Calvo and Mendoza, 2000) occurs when the market is uncertain about the skills of a particular manager. In case a fund manager makes an unfavorable decision, the negative effect on his reputation would be significantly lower, if others made the same "mistake" as well. Accordingly, for their reputation and thus their career, it is better for fund managers to "share the blame" with others and "hide in the herd" when their investment decisions emerge as being unprofitable.

Furthermore, their *compensation scheme* can motivate fund managers to mimic the actions of others, if they are evaluated in relation to a benchmark – typically versus a peer group or an appropriate index (Lakonishok et al., 1992, Maug and Naik, 1996, 2009). As *relative performance* measurement means that fund manager's compensation will be reduced if he underperforms his benchmark, he may seek to perform equally well or just follow his benchmark.[61]

Relative performance measurement is also likely to support some strategic behavior, which is not desirable on the part of fund managers' clients. Having to be (at least) as good as their benchmark/peers, herding fund managers may be motivated to reduce their *working effort,* as herding requires less effort on data research and analysis of investment opportunities. It would only require imitating the decisions of others (Lütje, 2009).

Finally, another potential reason for rational herd behavior in financial markets is *imperfect information* (Avery and Zemsky, 1998). In this model the assumptions are that all information relevant for the investment is public but there is uncertainty about the accuracy or quality of this information. Besides, there are two types of investors: Those who have very accurate private information, which may be conclusions of their research effort, and those who possess very noisy information. The latter may mimic the behavior of others, regardless of own private information, believing that the group they follow possesses more accurate information on the value of a security. In this case, an *information cascade* would start, i.e. an informational inefficient herd behavior, because it does not reflect the private information of trend followers (subsequent investors). Such herd behavior can lead to price bubbles and mispricing.

The assumption on the existence of informed and less informed investors fits best the situation in TM. We start the analysis on the motives for herd behavior by investigating whether the pronounced herding in TM is part of a price discovery process or whether it rather forms an information cascade.

---

61 In that case, fund manager's optimal investment portfolio would move closer to the benchmark's portfolio than if he was trading on his own account only.

Table 4.6 gives results for correlations and ordered PROBIT regressions of the answers to "I generally follow the trend" (proxies for a fund manager's degree of herding) and the six information sources described in the previous Section 4.6.2.

A result in favor of price discovery process would particularly be given by a positive correlation with the importance of fundamental information and discussion with colleagues. This would signalize that herding fund managers are interested in revealing fundamental values of their investment securities. Thus, they are less likely to fully disregard their own private information, gained from their own analysis and probably interpreted in discussions with colleagues. By contrast, a negative correlation with importance of fundamental information is more likely to mean that trend following is part of an information cascade[62]. In this case, a fund manager's buy or sell action is unlikely to reflect his private information. He would only follow the actions of his predecessors, believing that the majority of them has received more accurate signals about the security's value.

Contrary to the analysis on order flow, distinctive results between DM and TM occur in Table 4.6. Herding in DM goes along with higher orientation on least fundamental sources of information, i.e. mostly charts and technical indicators, other market players and opinion leading investment professionals, whereas fundamental facts and serious discussions with colleagues lose relevance. In TM the picture is different: Here, herding is significantly associated with fundamental orientation in Ukraine and orientation on economic opinion leaders in Russia. The correlation with technical analysis is only significant in Russia.

These results are even more focused in the ordered PROBIT regression. In DM, herd behavior is clearly determined by technical analysis and high orientation on opinion leaders of the asset management industry, but low orientation on fundamental information. Furthermore, the effect of other market players loses significance in the multivariate regression. Thus, observing their actions appears to be more relevant for the use of order flow, but less for herding.

62 "An invest cascade, say, starts with the first individual who finds that the number of predecessors who invested exceeds the predecessors who rejected by two", Bikhchandani and Sharma (2001), p. 286.

Table 4.6: Herd behavior and other information sources [(1)]

	Developed Markets		*Transition Markets*	
	USA	**GER**	**RUS**	**UA**
Coefficients of the Spearman Rank Correlation (p-value)	"I generally follow the trend"			
Fundamental facts about the company / market	**-0.315****** (0.000)**	**-0.254****** (0.000)**	-0.015 (0.893)	**0.403**** **(0.027)**
Discussions / exchange of views with colleagues	**-0.151*** **(0.068)**	**-0.116*** **(0.063)**	0.164 (0.132)	0.028 (0.881)
Statements of economic opinion leaders	0.102 (0.219)	0.051 (0.413)	**0.239**** **(0.027)**	0.136 (0.474)
Chart analysis / technical indicators	**0.372****** (0.000)**	**0.426****** (0.000)**	**0.412****** (0.000)**	0.219 (0.244)
Investment decision of other market players	**0.142*** **(0.085)**	**0.148**** **(0.017)**	-0.049 (0.654)	-0.119 (0.529)
Statements of opinion leaders within the industry	-0.014 (0.867)	**0.194****** (0.002)**	0.096 (0.381)	0.069 (0.716)
Coefficients of the ordered PROBIT regression (p-value)	"I generally follow the trend"			
Fundamental facts	**-0.244**** **(0.015)**	**-0.192**** **(0.012)**	-0.091 (0.423)	**1.065****** (0.002)**
Colleagues	-0.062 (0.422)	-0.074 (0.201)	0.156 (0.167)	0.047 (0.850)
Economic opinion leaders	0.040 (0.561)	-0.042 (0.458)	**0.235**** **(0.036)**	0.374 (0.153)
Chart analysis / technical indicators	**0.246****** (0.001)**	**0.306****** (0.000)**	**0.391****** (0.000)**	**0.302*** **(0.067)**
Other market players	0.051 (0.552)	0.034 (0.587)	-0.164 (0.182)	-0.126 (0.610)
Opinion leaders within the industry	-0.001 (0.989)	**0.126*** **(0.066)**	0.080 (0.490)	-0.209 (0.485)
Pseudo R^2	0.069	0.082	0.101	0.171
Number	145	263	86	30

(1) For the assessment of these sources of information, there are six answering categories, ranging from "highest relevance" (coded as 1) to "no relevance" (coded as 6).
Stars refer to level of significance: * 10%, ** 5%, *** 1%

However, besides the use of technical indicators, herd behavior in TM is driven by a substantial reliance on fundamental orientation in Ukraine (a coefficient of 1.065) and the attention to economic opinion leaders in Russia. In addition, contrary to DM, it is rather the reliance on discussions with colleagues and not the orientation on other market players, which initiates herd behavior in TM. Even though these results are not significant, they are in line with the message of significant ones.

To sum up, the analysis of characteristics in the information processing of herding fund managers indicates that herding in DM is likely to initiate information cascades (as herding fund managers' trades would not reveal their own private information). Contrary, herding fund managers in TM are less likely to mimic others by ignoring own private information due to their fundamental orientation. This point towards an effort on price discovery – a more efficient herd behavior, at least compared to DM.

4.6.4 Accessibility to order flow

Here we come back to the "puzzle" from Section 4.6.1: Whereas herd behavior is practiced rather by smaller companies in both DM and TM, order flow turns out to be relevant for smaller companies in DM, but for bigger ones in TM.

The size of an investment company (measured by assets under management) can be taken as proxy for the two investors' types in the market, i.e. informed and less informed ones, as e.g. defined in the theory on information cascades (Section 4.6.2). Keeping this in mind and combining our finding on the informational motives for using order flow and herding (Section 4.6.2-4.6.3) with the revealed institutional structures in the information processing (Section 4.6.1), we can explain the "puzzle" as follows.

In both DM and TM, small companies turn out to be trend "followers", although with different motivations. Consequently, trend "setters" are rather big companies, the group of well-informed investors with better private information due to their larger research capacities.

In DM, the interest of small companies in observing order flow and herding can be mainly justified by their research constraints. Thus, they aim to collect information from the actions' of other better-informed market players. In TM, small companies are fundamentally orientated trend followers, but they tend to rely less on order flow. Why? It would be implausible to assume lack of interest in this information category. It is rather a question of its accessibility.

The accessibility to order flow seems to be different in DM and TM. One rationale for this could be that order flow partly contains different information in

DM and TM. Especially in less transparent and less liquid TM, order flow is likely to subsume insider information (exploitation of which is not prosecuted in TM) on e.g. trading objectives of other big traders or planned trading orders of own company' clients. Thus, bigger companies have a better or even exclusive access to such information, making it profitable for them (by exploiting subsequent short-term price movements).

Second, order flow might be differently presented to market participants in DM and TM. In DM with strong prosecution of insider trading, order flow is typically observable in electronic trading systems, so that also small companies have access to it. Furthermore, as shown in Figure 4.1.B, the share of fund managers who pay attention to the order flow intraday is remarkably higher in TM, compared to DM. To profit from short-lived information during the course of a trading day, it requires high trading frequencies and a direct access to the market. In less liquid markets, both requirements are rather given in big companies.

Summing up, in contrast to herding, the reliance on the order flow seems not to complement fund managers' fundamental orientation, even not in less transparent TM. It rather enables bigger companies to profit from semi-fundamental information, predicting short-term price movements, which is especially pronounced in markets with limited trading as in Ukraine.

4.7 Motives for herding in DM and TM

We proceed by addressing motives for herd behavior in DM and TM. *Table 4.7* presents our findings from a multivariate regression of results to the statement "I generally follow the trend". It contains questionnaire statements which proxy for the relevant motivations documented in the literature and presented in Section 4.6.3.

The statement "Following the herd benefits career" indicates the relevance of reputational concerns for herding. Relative performance as bonus criterion catches the relevance of compensation schemes as herding motivation. Finally, fund managers' working effort is measured by their indicated average working hours per week. To account for further possible effects on herd behavior, we include some additional variables into our regression. First, these are the two distinctions in market settings of DM and TM which have been revealed in Section 4.4, i.e. the degree of short-term orientation and relevance assigned to absolute performance. Second, we also control for the kind of information processing when following trends by considering the relevance of fundamental information and chart analysis in our regression.

The results in Table 4.7 are evidently distinctive and provide further new insights: The three motives for herd behavior have the expected significant effects in DM, but not in TM. The more fund managers in the USA and Germany believe that herding benefits career and the less working effort they display, the more they tend to herd. Interestingly, relative performance evaluation does not significantly motivate to trend following in DM (at least in our sample). In addition, the incentive towards short-term performance orientation and thus high trading activity, which is set by their clients, also significantly promotes herd behavior. Finally, information processing related to herding is not fundamental, but technical. Summing up: "Hiding" in the herd due to career concerns and in order to reduce working effort as well as orientation on short-term performance turn out to be most pronounced motives for trend following in DM, whereas fundamental orientation loses relevance.

However, the picture is different in TM. We unveil following significant effects, being all contrary to DM: In Russia, bonus payments depending on relative performance and higher working effort promote herding. Furthermore, also the bonus incentive to perform well in absolute terms, being highly relevant in TM, triggers herd behavior. In Ukraine, the effects are mostly the same as in Russia, but not significant. This might be due to the small number of Ukrainian fund managers considered in this regression, as variables on bonus criteria reduce the Ukrainian sample to 15 respondents. However, a significant and even more important effect in the Ukrainian sample occurs with the variables controlling for information processing: Orientation on fundamental facts significantly promotes herd behavior – an effect which is even stronger than the one arising from technical analysis. This effect is also present in Russia, but is not significant for fundamentals.

Our results suggest that herding motives documented in the "Western" literature seem not (yet) to be crucial for trend following in TM, except for the relative performance in Russia. As herding in Eastern European TM is associated with higher working effort and fundamental orientation, it includes elements of efficient behavior – pointing towards fund mangers' effort for price discovery. These findings rather contradict herding in the sense of an information cascade or following trends by ignoring own private information (which is rather applicable to DM).

Table 4.7: Motives for herd behavior in DM and TM [(1)]

	Developed Markets		*Transition Markets*	
	USA	**GER**	**RUS**	**UA**
Coefficients of the ordered PROBIT regression (p-value)	"I generally follow the trend"			
Following the herd benefits career	**0.796***** **(0.000)**	**0.407***** **(0.000)**	0.230 (0.122)	0.516 (0.391)
Incentive: Relative performance	0.089 (0.376)	-0.041 (0.649)	**0.333**** **(0.029)**	0.092 (0.746)
Working effort	**-0.251*** **(0.060)**	**-0.208*** **(0.095)**	**0.291*** **(0.070)**	0.316 (0.479)
Pseudo R^2	0.092	0.030	0.043	0.034
Number	134	217	77	15
Additional variables [(2)] *(incentives)*				
Short-term performance	**0.600***** **(0.000)**	**0.342***** **(0.004)**	0.019 (0.908)	0.603 (0.216)
Absolute performance	-0.053 (0.619)	-0.062 (0.513)	**0.267*** **(0.067)**	-0.421 (0.274)
Pseudo R^2	0.136	0.054	0.060	0.088
Number	127	202	76	15
Additional variables [(3)] *(information)*				
Fundamental facts	**-0.468*** **(0.060)**	-0.197 (0.243)	0.138 (0.541)	**2.437**** **(0.043)**
Chart analysis / technical indicators	**0.378***** **(0.007)**	**0.766***** **(0.000)**	**0.674***** **(0.000)**	**1.075*** **(0.067)**
Pseudo R^2	0.179	0.144	0.119	0.278
Number	126	202	76	15

(1) For all statements there are six answering categories ranging from "completely agree" or "highest relevance" (coded as 1) to "complete disagree" or "no relevance" (coded as 6). Working hours per week are indicated by six answering categories: <41 (coded as 1); 41-45; 46-50; 51-55; 56-60; >60 (coded as 6). The coefficients for 'working effort' are multiplied by (-1) to simplify interpretation.

(2) To the well-known motives for herding mentioned above, we add additional variables to improve the explanatory power of the regression. By doing so, the variable 'working effort' loses its significance in Germany.

(3) By adding the two information categories to the regression, the variable 'absolute performance' remains close to significance with a p-value of (0.111).

Stars refer to level of significance: * 10%, ** 5%, *** 1%

4.8 Conclusion

This paper provides supportive survey evidence for the hypothesis that fund managers' information processing differs between Western developed markets (DM) and Eastern European transition markets (TM). These markets are characterized by dissimilar market settings, regarding transparency and information availability (thus costs of information acquisition), market liquidity, institutional development, and regulatory restrictions.

Comparing survey evidence of 528 fund managers from the USA and Germany (DM) as well as Russia and Ukraine (TM), reveals several pronounced differences on fund managers' information processing. Starting with the comparative relevance of the three basic information categories in the asset management (i.e. fundamental facts, technical analysis, and order flow): In DM, fundamental information gains highest relevance for investment decision-marking, whereby especially the order flow (as non-fundamental information category) remarkably loses consideration. In contrast, in TM fundamental information loses relevance mostly in favor of order flow observation. Furthermore, TM stand out due to their high level of trend following. Besides, fund managers in TM state a comparatively higher orientation towards short-term performance and assign a strikingly higher relevance to absolute performance (as bonus criterion) compared to their peers in DM.

The revealed features of TM, i.e. high relevance assigned to order flow and high level of herding, are assumed to reduce market efficiency from the point of view of DM. In this context, it would be desirable for market efficiency to identify these TM-characteristics as part of a price discovery process in markets, where information is priced more slowly. Indeed, we find supportive fundamental orientation for herd behavior in Russia and particularly in Ukraine. In contrast, in both DM and TM, order flow analysis lacks fundamental orientation, suggesting it to contain rather short-lived, semi-fundamental private information.

Furthermore, the influence of company size on fund managers' information processing differs between DM and TM. In DM, rather smaller companies tend to both, observing order flow and following trends (herding). Interestingly, in TM, these are smaller companies who follow trends, but bigger ones who are more interested in the order flow – probably due to their privileged access to it and their higher trading frequencies. This would further confirm order flow to contain rather short-lived semi-fundamental information (about trading objectives of large own clients or other traders).

Apart from this, we also find Eastern European fund managers to generally resemble their peers in developed Western markets in several aspects (e.g.

perception of information advantages, view on the market, time invested in research).

In sum, we derive two important implications from our study. First, inasmuch market prices are likely to be influenced by fund managers' investment decisions which in turn result from their information processing, our insights into the latter contribute to a better understanding of price movements in both, DM and TM. Thereby, particularly our evidence for Russia and Ukraine is new so far. Second and fortunately, our results reduce the concerns which may appear at first glance regarding the relatively high reliance on non-fundamental information in TM: We find some supportive evidence for efficient elements in trend following in TM. This might indicate an effort for price discovery. However, we also show that the quality of an investment environment significantly affects fund managers' information processing. Thus, to promote efficiency, which reduces the need for costly private information acquisition and thus the relevance of non-fundamental information, the investment environment in TM has to be further improved. Given a more effective regulation and appropriate disclosure enforcement mechanisms, the revealed characteristics of Eastern European fund managers are likely to further contribute to market efficiency.

5 Fund managers' investment behavior in different market settings: Evidence from Russia, Thailand, and Germany[63]

5.1 Introduction

The global expansion of the asset management industry is reflected in its huge capital inflows and growing numbers of asset management companies. Meanwhile, this applies not only to developed, but also to emerging markets. Thus, fund managers of mutual or pension funds manage steadily growing volumes of assets, which underpins the influence of their asset allocation decisions on securities markets (cf. Ong and Sy, 2004).

The notable research interest on institutional investors during the past two decades has been motivated by these actors' increasing relevance not only for domestic markets, but also worldwide. They have become important contributors to the financial market integration, thereby also bringing destabilization risks to emerging markets during recent crises, i.e. international mutual funds' large withdrawals from emerging regions (Aitken, 1998, Kaminsky et al., 2001, Gelos and Wei, 2005). Most studies on institutional investors concentrate on aggregated fund flow analyses by investigating mutual fund performance, strategies and price impact.[64] Thereby, findings also indicate

---

63 I would like to thank my co-author Daniela Beckmann. We are grateful to all the fund managers in Russia, Thailand, and Germany who participated in the survey and who were available as interview partners. Besides, financial support by the VolkswagenStiftung is highly appreciated. Moreover, we thank the Russian National League of Asset Managers "NLU", the Thai Association of Investment Management Companies "AIMC", and the German Investment Association "BVI" for great recommendation letters and organizational support. Finally, helpful comments by Lukas Menkhoff and Maik Schmeling as well as great research assistance by Torben Lütje are gratefully acknowledged.

64 While the majority of studies focus on U.S. institutional investors (cf. e.g. Lakonishok et al., 1992, Grinblatt et al., 1995, Carhart, 1997, Wermers, 1999, or Sias, 2004), considerably fewer studies address the Japanese or the European mutual fund industry (cf. e.g. Cai et al. 1997, Otten and Bams, 2002, or Walter and Weber, 2006). Regarding mutual funds in emerging markets, studies concentrate on transactions data explorations of mainly U.S. hosted mutual funds operating in emerging markets: Disyatat and Gelos (2001), Kaminsky et al. (2001) or Ong and Sy (2004) focus on a better understanding of funds' portfolio choice and its impact in a broad set of emerging markets. Borensztein and Gelos (2003) and Kaminsky et al. (2004) address mutual fund strategies, and find evidence for momentum strategies, i.e. the systematic selling of losers and buying of

mutual fund investments to be biased when recognizing anomalies such as "herd behavior", first modeled by Schafstein and Stein (1990), or the so-called "home bias", early documented by French and Poterba (1991). However, empirical micro-level studies on the individual fund manager's investment process remain comparably scarce – particularly in emerging markets.

This paper intends to fill this gap to some extent by providing comparative evidence on fund managers' investment behavior in different market environments. In so doing, we test the hypothesis that fund managers from emerging markets behave more biased than do their peers from developed markets. This is likely to be the case assuming that an emerging investment environment might induce more biased investment actions due to e.g. its lower market transparency and information efficiency or its scarce professional training opportunities. A questionnaire survey among professional asset managers from the emerging markets Russia and Thailand as well as the developed one Germany allows us to shed light on the above hypothesis.[65] We test for differences in fund managers' risk propensity and behavior, as the basis for every investment decision, as well as in their propensity to two of the most discussed behavioral biases, herd behavior and home-biased asset allocation. Besides, for the latter two biases we also analyze the relevance of their underlying motives documented in the literature and control for possible effects arising from fund managers' personal characteristics and risk-related personal biases.

The role of individual fund managers has been mainly explored in the U.S. mutual fund industry. Prominent studies by e.g. Chevalier and Ellison (1999a, 1999b) relate fund managers' performance and herd behavior to their personal characteristics such as age, professional experience and education. They find that fund manager's experience has a significant positive effect on his fund's performance, which is also confirmed by e.g. Ding and Wermers (2007). Furthermore, gender-related effects occur when regarding investment styles and performance distribution, as shown by Niessen and Ruenzi (2009). For the European mutual fund industry, knowledge concerning individual asset managers' behavior has been largely complemented by survey studies, such as Menkhoff (1997), Arnswald (2001), or Menkhoff et al. (2006) for the German

winners, as well as significant but moderate herd behavior of emerging markets funds. Choe et al. (1999) and Kim and Wei (2002), who focus on the Korean stock market, detect positive feedback trading, i.e. momentum investment, and herd behavior of non-resident institutional investors.

65 Studies on asset managers in Germany and Thailand by Lütje and Menkhoff (2007) and Beckmann et al. (2008) rely on the same survey.

market. Asian emerging markets have been addressed by e.g. Beckmann et al. (2008) or Fischer et al. (2009).

Research on emerging markets funds is usually motivated by their different investment environment compared to developed markets, resulting from their industry's special history or a different market development stage. Particularly, emerging financial markets can be distinguished by scarcity of publicly available information, high asymmetric information distribution and, thus, often less transparency compared to developed financial markets. At the same time, their institutional and regulatory framework is comparably less developed (Beim and Calomiris, 2001). Such different market rules might induce a change / adjustment in market participants' behavior, implying potentially more biased actions. For example, limited information access could lead to a stronger orientation on other market players. Indeed, the neglect of the own (limited) information in favor of following better-informed market players' actions could even be rational (cf. Bikhchandani and Sharma, 2001).

Empirical evidence suggests the quality of an investment environment to affect its consideration in international portfolios. Ahearne et al. (2004) aim to explain the home bias in equity holdings of U.S. portfolios. They find the quality of provided financial information in foreign markets to be decisive for foreign investments of U.S. investors. The latter significantly less underweight foreign countries whose firms underlie the U.S. regulatory requirements by public U.S. listing – thus reducing information asymmetries. To examine the relevance of market transparency for international funds' investments, Gelos and Wei (2005) measure government and corporate transparency in several countries and find that international emerging market funds invest systematically less in less transparent countries. Moreover, some evidence also indicates that foreign institutional investors' propensity to exit non-transparent markets is higher during crises. Aggarwal et al. (2005) reveal the quality of accounting standards, shareholder rights, information disclosure and legal frameworks to be of significant relevance for non-resident emerging market funds' allocation.

Our results broadly support our hypothesis by revealing asset managers in emerging markets to indicate a significantly more biased behavior compared to their German peers. This applies to the risk-related biases loss aversion and disposition effect as well as to herd behavior and, most pronounced, the home bias. However, general risk aversion does not seem to depend on market development, as we unveil both the sample's highest (Thailand) and lowest (Russia) risk aversion in our emerging markets sample. In the analysis of the motives for herding, we find supportive evidence for the prominent motives from the literature (e.g. reputation concerns) and additionally reveal risk-related biases, i.e. risk and loss aversion as well as the disposition effect, to have a positive influence on herd behavior. Hence, we find a rational background for herding in our sample. Interestingly, another relevant result is that herding asset managers from emerging markets pay a higher attention to fundamental information than their German peers. Our analysis of the home bias mostly indicates the predominance of regulatory restrictions in emerging markets, where the average fund manager would allocate a strikingly high investment share to his respective home market. However, particularly in emerging markets, also a better level of information on the home market compared to that on foreign markets may partly explain home market investments. Moreover, the risk-related biases disposition effect and loss aversion are found to have significant effects on the home bias, whereas loss aversion is particularly influential in the two emerging markets. Besides, the preference for the home market is more pronounced among female fund managers in the two emerging markets.

Hence, our contribution to the literature is threefold. First, we provide new data that allows to obtain insights on individual asset managers' behavior, being so far scarce for Asian and, particularly, for Eastern European emerging markets. Second, we extend the research on the features of mutual fund industries in emerging and developed markets by revealing important differences in individual characteristics, views, risk and investment behavior between fund managers from Russia, Thailand, and Germany. The supposition that fund managers in emerging investment environments might behave relatively more cautious and/or more biased becomes easily accepted regarding the poor information availability, low market transparency as well as less training and career development opportunities in emerging markets. Third and finally, we extend the evidence and (risk-related) motivation analysis for two prominent behavioral biases: Herd behavior and home bias.

The remainder of this paper is organized as follows. Section 5.2 briefly informs about the development of our three selected markets. Section 5.3 describes our generated data set, its representativeness as well as our surveyed fund managers' personal characteristics. Section 5.4 presents evidence for risk-related behavior, being crucial for investment decisions. A more detailed analysis of herd behavior and the home bias is provided in Section 5.5 and Section 5.6, respectively. Section 5.7 concludes.

5.2 Investment industries in Russia, Thailand, and Germany

Describing our three selected markets, we find the comparatively young Russian asset management industry to have experienced an exceptional growth in the years 2003 to 2007, regarding company and fund number as well as fund inflows. In 2003, the annual growth rate of Russian funds' net asset value displayed 506%, indicating a jump from RUB 13 billion (bn) to RUB 77bn (USD 2.7bn) within just one year. The annual growth rates of the following four years varied between 33% and 120%, resulting in a net asset value of RUB 406bn (USD 15bn) in 2006 and RUB 730bn (USD 30.5bn) in 2007. Since the beginning of 2003, such growth thus results in a five-years-growth-rate of over 5,670%. This dynamic has been vastly dominated by the growth of closed-end funds, which managed 77% (USD 23.5 bn) of Russian net assets in 2007. Thereby, the asset classes equity and real estate each accounted for one third of closed-end funds' assets. The assets of open-end funds amounted to RUB 11.9bn (USD 0.4bn) in 2002, RUB 150bn (USD 5.6bn) in 2006 and RUB 176bn (USD 7.3bn) in 2007. However, since the crisis year 2008, the annual growth rates of the whole industry have declined to -30%, so that in the beginning of 2010, the net asset value of Russian funds added up to RUB 322bn (USD 10.7bn), of which RUB 96bn (USD 3.2bn) are managed in open-end funds. In 2010, there are over 430 asset management companies in Russia.[66] The Thai mutual fund industry has grown by at least 20% annually since 2002, summing up to almost THB 1,122bn (USD 30bn) of net assets in September 2006.[67] In contrast to that, the German asset management industry in total keeps track on a steady and comparatively less exceptional growth path: since 2002, assets under management grew by at least 4.5 % annually from 862.4 billion EUR (904 billion USD) to 1,205 billion EUR (1,545 billion USD) in 2006.[68]

During our survey period (see Section 5.3), mutual fund investment instruments in both considered emerging markets ranged from fixed income funds to money market, equity and balanced or mixed funds, as well as indexed

66 Data is taken from "Market Statistics" provided by the "NLU" (Russian National League of Asset Managers) on its homepage.

67 Numbers are provided by the "AIMC" (Thai Association of Investment Management Companies). At the time we were conducting our survey, additional private and provident funds taken together added another two third of the mutual funds' volume to the total of net asset value managed by Thai asset management companies.

68 Data is taken from the annual reports of the German Investment Management Association 'BVI'. Numbers comprise round about 50% mutual funds, and 50% restricted/special funds (German 'Spezialfonds').

funds and funds of funds in Russia and so-called flexible portfolio funds in Thailand. In Germany, mutual fund investment options included real estate and others, e.g. commodities, in addition. A noticeable difference linked to the industry's development appears, when regarding institutional and regulatory restrictions: In comparison to German asset management companies that could offer a broad range of globally investing funds to their customers, asset management companies in Russia and Thailand faced clearly higher restrictions regarding investment abroad. In Russia, mutual funds are legally allowed to invest up to 20 percent of their assets in foreign shares and bonds. However, until 2008, Russian asset management companies have not been able to buy foreign assets because the latter have not been defined by the Russian law. Besides, the operational system for investing abroad was not properly settled.[69] In Thailand, only five companies were licensed to offer so-called foreign-invested funds.

5.3 Survey data

Our data comprehends 476 questionnaires, originating from an international written survey project in the Thai and German asset management industry between spring 2003 and spring 2005 and the Russian asset management industry in 2008. In particular, we questioned professional asset managers about their market views and behavior.

Survey studies have the advantage of offering a direct measure of individual attitudes instead of having to rely on assumptions about individual behavior. Nevertheless, they occasionally face criticism in terms of data quality, target group choice and strategic answering. In order to overcome possible skepticism, we did not only prepare our survey by previous oral interviews with asset managers from different investment companies in several German cities, Bangkok, and Moscow, but also assured in test runs that questions and response categories were well understood and in common wording. Moreover, for planned cross-country comparisons, questions had to be both relevant for the

69 In November 2007, the Russian Federal Service for Financial Markets has published a list of foreign shares, bonds and investment funds' that can be used as investment tools by Russian mutual funds and non-governmental pension funds to improve their portfolio diversification. Traders agree that the development of investing in foreign securities will depend on the real demand from investors. However, there is no consensus on when the latter will appear. It might be soon, if e.g. thinking of attractive investments in the BRIC countries, but also in a few years, if the Russian market will continue generating returns on par with developed markets.

respective market and, if necessary, country-specifically adapted, but still comparable afterwards. Finally, guaranteed anonymity to all participants helped to overcome possible objections, and as in a market sample of over hundred questionnaires the marginal influence of a single person is obviously limited, incentives for strategic answering have been low.
Altogether, we obtained a participation rate of 68.7%[70] of contacted investment companies *(Table 5.1)*. In detail, in Russia, 58 of 104[71] contacted companies managing (open-end) mutual funds contributed to our survey (participation rate of Russian firms: 55.7%). Out of these 58, seven investment companies belong to the fifteen biggest market players. A supporting letter by the investment association "NLU" – the Russian National League of Asset Managers – was the key to success for our survey in Russia. In Thailand, we received responses from 29 of 31 contacted member companies of the "AIMC" – the Thai Association of Investment Management Companies (participation rate of Thai firms: 93.6%). Regarding assets under management, our survey covers more than 96% of the Thai market. The extraordinary high participation rate is attributable to recommendation and helpful support of the "AIMC". In Germany, 51 of 66 addressed investment companies participated in our survey (participation rate of German firms: 77.3%). As almost all big market players took part in our survey, market coverage in terms of assets under management sums up to 92%. All companies are member firms of the German Investment Management Association "BVI", and, once more, the association's letter of recommendation supported high participation rates.

Bigger investment companies with higher asset volumes under management typically employ more asset managers and therefore have a bigger market impact than smaller investment firms. We test whether our sample is representative in this respect as well. Correlation coefficients between number of answered questionnaires and company size are positive, ranging between 0.2 and 0.7. This confirms that asset managers who work for bigger companies participated significantly more in our survey.

---

70 Similar surveys by e.g. Shiller and Pound (1989), Oberlechner (2001), Gehrig and Menkhoff (2004), or Menkhoff and Schmidt (2005) report company participation rates of 45%, 54%, 51%, and 59%, respectively.

71 At the time we started conducting our survey in Russia, total fund assets have been managed by 284 investment companies. Out of these, open-end mutual funds have been offered by 109 companies.

Table 5.1: Comparison of the data sample with the industry structure [(a)]

	Russia	Thailand	Germany
Number of received questionnaires	87	126	263
Firm participation rate	55.7%	93.6%	77.3%
Covered market share (by assets under management)	40.8%	96.5%	91.8%
	Correlation [(b)] with company size (by assets under management)		
Number of answered questionnaires per company	0.240^{*} (0.077)	0.534^{***} (0.000)	0.679^{***} (0.000)

(a) For Russia, we use market data (on companies managing open-end mutual funds) provided by the NLU for the year 2008. The market data for Thailand is taken from a market share datasheet provided by selected companies of the Thai asset management industry and private information provided by the AIMC. We refer to June and July 2004 as months of reference. For Germany, market data is taken from the annual report 2003 of the BVI.

(b) The table gives the coefficient of the Pearson correlation with the p-value in parentheses. Stars refer to level of significance: * 10%, ** 5%, *** 1%

Asset managers' characteristics are shown in *Table 5.2*. Over all three countries, the average asset manager is 35 years old, has seven years of professional experience, works as senior asset manager, holds a higher educational degree, and is male and most probably married.

When taking a closer look, however, expected differences from a perspective of developmental progress between the two emerging markets and the more mature one, as well as country-related particularities become evident. First of all, in accordance with market and industry history and development, we find clearly more young asset managers in Russia, i.e. 45.3% younger than 31 years (and even 28% younger than 27). Also, there are more fund managers with long professional experience, i.e. more than 12 years, in the German market than in the Thai sub-sample. The conspicuous high number of Russian asset managers with professional experience over 10 years is in line with an exceptionally high participation (48%) of Russian asset managers in leading positions.[72] Concerning education, the number of asset managers with a master or PhD degree is exceptionally high in Russia and Thailand, while Germany meets expectations.

72 This is highly appreciated from the perspective of capturing relevant market actors with our data.

Table 5.2: Personal characteristics of surveyed asset managers [a)]

Age (in years)	*< 31*	*31 – 35*	*36 – 40*	*41 – 45*	*> 45*	Mean	N
RUS	45,3%	25.6%	19.8%	4.7%	4.7%	~33	86
TH	16.7%	36.5%	33.3%	11.9%	1.6%	~35	126
GER	21.0%	35.5%	22.9%	14.9%	5.7%	~36	262
Professional experience (in years) [b)]	*< 3*	*3 – 6*	*7 – 8*	*9 – 10*	*> 10*	Mean	
	23.3%	29.1%	11.6%	8.1%	27.9%	~ 7	
	< 4	*4 – 6*	*7 – 9*	*10 – 12*	*> 12*		
	24.6%	19.0%	27.8%	20.6%	7.9%	~ 7	
	32.0%	20.7%	19.1%	10.9%	17.2%	~ 7	
Occupational level	*Junior AM*		*Senior AM*		*Head of AM team*	*CIO/CEO*	
	5.8%		46.5%		31.4%	16.3%	
	38.1%		45.2%		11.9%	4.8%	
	32.0%		46.1%		16.4%	5.5%	
Educational level	*Bachelor*	*Master or PhD*	Bonus payments	*Median*		*Std. dev.*	
	-	24.7% (75.3%) [c)]		50.0%		78,6	
	4.0%	96.0%		16.0%		47.8	
	13.2%	86.6%		25.0%		24.0	
Gender	*Male*	*Female*	Marital status	*Single*	*Married*	*Other*	
	94.3%	5.7%		31.0%	69.0%	0.0%	
	53.6%	46.4%		55.9%	43.0%	1.1%	
	90.0%	10.0%		44.1%	53.5%	2.4%	

(a) Regarding each item, the first row displays responses of Russian asset managers, the second row those of Thai and the third row those of German asset managers.

(b) Acting on Russian fund managers' advice given in our pre-survey interviews, here, we have adopted the answering categories to better capture fund managers' age in the comparatively young Russian fund market. That is why the answering categories in Russia differ from those in Thailand and Germany.

(c) For Russia, the answer categories for educational level differ from those in other markets to correspond the Russian educational system. The parenthesis gives the share of answers for the category "highest", meaning Russian highest university degree (Diploma), which is comparable to a Master degree. The Bachelor/Master degrees have only recently been introduced in Russia.

Country specific differences are most obvious regarding gender and marital status: While Russian asset managers are overwhelmingly male and married, asset managers in Thailand are almost 50% female and, independent from gender in the majority single. Typically, (male) German asset managers are almost equally single and married.

5.4 Risk behavior

Undoubtedly, the investor's risk propensity is essential to every investment decision she takes. While standard finance theory assumes the individual investor to be generally risk averse – modeled by concavity of the utility function and expressed by the risk premium as compensation for risk taking – differences in the individual investor's degree of risk aversion imply different proportionate allocations between investment choices.

Risk aversion is linked to two other risk-related behavioral phenomena. Prospect theory, developed by Kahneman and Tversky's (1979), revises assumptions of the traditional expected utility framework and introduces the concept of *"loss aversion"*, expressed as utility functions with concavity in the domain of gains and convexity in the domain of losses - relative to a reference point (cf. Schmidt and Zank, 2005, for an overview and analogies to risk aversion). Indeed, investors seem to be less sensitive to gains than they are to losses: Empirical evidence shows that the latter is weighted twice as strongly (cf. Tversky and Kahnemann, 1992). Besides, there is wide acceptance that investors undergo a so-called *"disposition effect"* in their investment decision behavior. The tendency to hold losing stocks too long and to sell winning stocks too early was first reported by Shefrin and Statman (1985). Since then, empirical studies have largely confirmed it for both, individual and institutional investors (cf. e.g. Odean, 1998, Grinblatt and Keloharju, 2001, Shapira and Venezia, 2001, Garvey and Murphy, 2004, Locke and Mann, 2005). Again, prospect theory provides the explanatory description: Relying on an S-shaped value function, risk aversion in the gain domain causes the investors to realize profits quickly in order to avoid them turning into losses, while risk-seeking behavior in the loss domain lets losses run in hope of asset price recovery and the avoidance of any losses at all.

We therefore start our analysis of asset managers' behavior in the three countries by directly surveying their self-assessment for their risk behavior. *Table 5.3* reveals the distribution of answers for the three countries.

First, we are interested in their general *risk aversion* in respect to professional investment decisions (statement [1]). Whereas a clear majority of the Thai asset managers (64%) indicates to act mostly risk averse, only 48% of the German asset managers do so. However, lowest risk-aversion is stated in the Russian sample (share of agreement: 37%), where 21% declare to be only little risk-averse (answering categories 5 and 6).

Table 5.3: Asset managers' risk aversion, loss aversion and disposition affect [(a)]

Different dimensions of risk behavior [1]-[3]		Very risk avers / complete agreement (in %) 1	2	3	4	5	Little risk averse / complete disagreement (in %) 6	% of risk / loss averse AM [(b)]	Mean	Median
[1] In respect of professional investment decisions, I mostly act… (Risk aversion)	Russia	1.2	10.6	24.7	42.4	16.5	4.7	36.5%	3.8	4
	Thailand	1.6	25.4	36.5	27.0	8.7	0.8	63.5%	3.2	3
	Germany	1.5	9.2	36.9	42.7	8.5	1.2	47.6%	3.5	4
[2] In case of loss positions in my portfolio I generally wait for a price rebound instead of selling those securities. (Loss aversion)	Russia	3.5	17.4	20.9	14.0	25.6	18.6	41.8%	4.0	4
	Thailand	0.8	14.4	33.6	24.8	22.4	4.0	48.8%	3.7	4
	Germany	0.0	4.6	19.7	17.8	30.1	27.8	24.3%	4.6	5
[3] I prefer to take profits instead of cutting losses, when I am confronted with unexpected liquidity demands. (Disposition effect)	Russia	5.9	16.5	21.2	17.6	23.5	15.3	43.6%	3.8	4
	Thailand	5.6	38.1	23.0	12.7	14.3	6.3	66.7%	3.1	3
	Germany	3.5	12.0	22.4	15.4	21.6	25.1	37.9%	4.2	4

H_0: No specific difference between … [(c)]

	all three markets	*GER vs. RUS*	*GER vs. TH*	*RUS vs. TH*
[1]	**20.155*** (0.000)**	**-2.177*** (0.029)**	**-3.397*** (0.001)**	**-4.002*** (0.000)**
[2]	**44.574*** (0.000)**	**-3.228*** (0.001)**	**-6.630*** (0.000)**	**-1.663* (0.096)**
[3]	**41.148*** (0.000)**	**-1.751* (0.080)**	**-6.387*** (0.000)**	**-3.516*** (0.000)**

(a) For each statement, there are six answering categories, ranging from "very risk-averse" / "complete agreement" (coded as 1) to "little risk-averse" / "complete disagreement" (6). Thus, a mean of 3.5 or less indicates rather approval to the statement.

(b) The percentages given are calculated as the sum of the first three answering categories.

(c) The table gives the chi-squared value of the Kruskal-Wallis-test regarding the responses from all three markets and the z-value of the Mann-Whitney U-test regarding the markets pairwise, respectively. The p-values are given in parentheses.

Stars refer to level of significance: * 10%, ** 5%, *** 1%

Second, in case of loss positions in their portfolio (statement [2]), 42% of the Russian and 49% of the Thai asset managers would rather wait for a price rebound instead of selling those securities. In Germany, only 24% of the surveyed asset managers reveal this kind of *loss aversion*.

Third, we survey the existence of investors' *disposition* between winning and losing assets (statement [3]). In a situation of unexpected liquidity demands, 44% of the Russian asset managers prefer to take profits instead of cutting losses. In Thailand, these are even 67%. By contrast, the share of agreement on statement [3] is only 38% in the German sample.

Thus, especially with respect to the behavioral anomalies loss aversion and disposition effect, addressed in statements [2] and [3], we find asset managers in both emerging markets to be more biased than their German counterparts. In order to test for significant differences, in its lower part Table 5.3 also indicates the Kruskal-Wallis-tests for the whole sample as well as the Mann-Whitney U-tests for pairwise comparisons of markets regarding each of the three statements. In all three risk dimensions, test results confirm significant differences between all markets respectively, being most pronounced between Thailand and Germany. Even though asset managers in the two emerging markets Russia and Thailand tend to deviate from the German ones in the same direction, they do also significantly differ in their risk attitudes. Therefore, for our further analysis, we will regard the sample from the developed German market as a reference group, and will compare the two emerging markets rather separately (than pooled) to it.

It has been shown – especially by psychological research – that risk attitude and behavior also depend on personal characteristics such as gender or experience. Hence, we control for these characteristics in addition. Thereby, we also meet the demand to consider countries' peculiarities in our samples. As described in Section 5.3, sample differences emerge for the highly correlated characteristics experience, age, marital status and position[73], as well as in regards to gender.

Table 5.4 discloses linkages between risk behavior and *personal characteristics* with the help of Spearman rank correlation coefficients.

73 Considering experience as the most meaningful variable out of these four, we concentrate on it in the following. For more detailed correlations cf. Table 4, footnote b.

Table 5.4: Findings on risk behavior and personal characteristics

Correlations with risk behavior	Spearman rank correlation coefficients (p-value) [(a)]								
	Risk aversion			Loss aversion			Disposition effect		
	RUS	*TH*	*GER*	*RUS*	*TH*	*GER*	*RUS*	*TH*	*GER*
Female					0.176** (0.050)			0.154* (0.086)	0.128** (0.041)
Experience [(b)]								-0.215*** (0.015)	-0.147** (0.020)

(a) Only significant rank correlation coefficients are shown here.

(b) In all three countries experience is highly correlated with other asset managers' characteristics (Table 5.2). Spearman rank correlation coefficients are as follows on age: RUS: 0.636**, TH: 0.636***, GER: 0.744***; position: RUS: 0.445***, TH: 0.641***, GER: 0.511***; and marital status: RUS: 0.461***, TH: 0.353***, GER: 0.428***.

Stars refer to level of significance: * 10%, ** 5%, *** 1%

In Russia, we do not observe any significant results. By contrast, in Thailand, loss aversion seems to be more pronounced among female asset managers, while a higher disposition effect is significantly related to less experience. In Germany, the disposition effect is significantly correlated with both, gender and experience.[74] We concentrate on these two as control variables when addressing further investment biases related to fund managers' risk and loss attitudes.

First, e.g. Khorana (1996), Graham (1999) or Hong et al. (2000) interpret a higher degree of herd behavior as lower risk taking induced by reputation and career concerns as well as the fear of worse performance in relation to the peer group. Moreover, empirical work has shown that younger and more inexperienced asset managers tend to herd more often, as they are more at risk to be replaced for a worse performance than their older, more experienced colleagues (Chevalier and Ellison, 1999b, Arora and Ou-Yang, 2001).

Second, a home-biased asset allocation implies the waiving of advantages from international diversification, which may seem risk seeking from the perspective of expected utility. Behavioral explanations, however, such as perceived competence (cf. Kilka and Weber, 2000), shed light on the link between individual risk aversion and a home-biased asset allocation that might at least be perceived less risky by the individual investor (cf. Weber et al.,

74 The two variables also matter when controlled simultaneously in a multivariate framework for Thailand and Germany. Results are not explicitly shown here.

2005). Hence, we now turn to the two behavioral biases herd behavior and home bias, while searching for their influential factors and controlling for personal characteristics as well as risk-related behavior.

5.5 Herd behavior

Providing comprehensive survey work, Bikhchandani and Sharma (2001) distinguish spurious from intentional herd behavior in the market. As only the obvious intent to copy the behavior of others should be seen critical, we concentrate on the second type of herding. Three explanations of the latter are provided and have received overwhelming research attention. The first is the idea of *reputation-based herding*, first modeled by Scharfstein and Stein (1990). They regard herding as an agency phenomena joined with market's uncertainty about the manager's skills. Investment professionals have an incentive for "sharing-the-blame" and "hiding in the herd" if they fear negative consequences of unprofitable investment decisions. The latter weigh less in case other managers make the same 'mistakes', too. Reputation-based herding has been empirically confirmed by e.g. Chevalier and Ellison (1999b) and Hong et al. (2000). Second, affiliated to the former explanation, *compensation-based herding* can occur if investor's compensation depends on her investment performance relative to the performance of other investors, i.e. her benchmark – a remuneration scheme that is often applied in asset management. As her total compensation decreases in case of underperformance, the investor has a strong incentive to move closest to the benchmark by imitating others (Maug and Naik, 1996). Hence, in all three kinds of herding it can be rational from the individual asset manager's perspective to ignore privately received information signals and to prioritize copying the behavior of other market players (cf. also Devenow and Welch, 1996, for an overview of rational herd behavior in financial markets). The third explanation addresses *information-based* herding that is attributable to the occurrence of information cascades (cf. Bikhchandani et al., 1992). In a surrounding of imperfect information, investors are only able to observe the behavior of other market participants, but not the private information the latter receive. As soon as the observed behavior of others seems slightly more informative than the own private signals, investors are likely to neglect own information and copy the others instead.

Table 5.5: Evidence on herd behavior [(a)]

[1] Perception of herd behavior and [2] own trend following		Complete agreement (in %) 1	2	3	4	5	Complete disagreement (in %) 6	% of agreement (b)	Mean	Median
[1] Herding is observable amongst professional asset managers.	Russia	9.2	28.7	35.6	14.9	8.0	3.4	73.5%	2.9	3
	Thailand	3.2	35.2	41.6	12.8	4.8	2.4	80.0%	2.9	3
	Germany	20.5	46.4	24.3	2.7	2.3	3.8	91.2%	2.3	2
[2] I generally follow the trend.	Russia	15.1	31.4	29.1	14.0	5.8	4.7	75.6%	2.8	3
	Thailand	3.2	23.0	32.5	24.6	12.7	4.0	58.7%	3.3	3
	Germany	2.3	13.5	34.4	24.3	17.0	8.5	50.2%	3.7	3

H_0: No specific difference between … (c)

	all three markets	*GER vs. RUS*	*GER vs. TH*	*RUS vs. TH*
[1]	**45.277*** (0.000)**	**-4.880*** (0.000)**	**-5.865*** (0.000)**	-0.311 (0.755)
[2]	**32.502*** (0.000)**	**-5.548*** (0.000)**	**-2.450** (0.014)**	**-3.342*** (0.001)**

(a) For each statement, there are six answering categories, ranging from "complete agreement" (coded as 1) to "complete disagreement" (6). Thus, a mean of 3.5 or less indicates rather approval to the statement.

(b) The percentages given are calculated as the sum of the first three answering categories.

(c) The table gives the chi-squared value of the Kruskal-Wallis-test regarding the responses from all three markets and the z-value of the Mann-Whitney U-test regarding the markets pairwise, respectively. The p-values are given in parentheses.

Stars refer to level of significance: * 10%, ** 5%, *** 1%

We start our analysis of herd behavior in emerging and developed market environments by providing evidence of its existence *(Table 5.5)*. On the one hand, we ask our respondents whether they perceive herding amongst professional asset managers (statement [1]). On the other hand, we request an indication of their own trend following behavior, which serves to detect their degree of herding (statement [2]). General agreement on *observable herding* is lowest among the Russian fund managers with 74%, amounts to 80% among the Thai asset managers, and peaks at 91% among the German asset managers. In contrast to their perception of herding in the market, German asset managers themselves indicate least to follow the trend. Only 50% of them agree on *own trend following*, and 8.5% even completely reject it. Among surveyed Thai asset managers, 59% agree on trend following. An outstanding result is revealed in the Russian sample, where the share of trend followers sums up to 76%, and 15.1% of fund managers even completely agree (highest agreement category) to follow the trend. Hence, only Russian fund managers perceive herding in the market to the same degree as they state to follow trends themselves.

The Mann-Whitney U-tests confirm the revealed differences between the German asset managers and those from both emerging markets to be significant. On the other hand, the test supports the similarity in the perception of herding between Russia and Thailand.

This immediately raises the follow-up question of the *motives for herd behavior.* In order to get a first idea of what might motivate surveyed professionals to herd and whether they differ in diverging market environments, we, again, compare the Russian and Thai samples to the German one. *Figure 5.1* displays mean answers, categorized by own trend following behavior, to three statements aiming to address reputation, compensation, and information based causes of herd behavior as described in the literature.

Starting with the relevance of *reputational concerns*, it depends on how asset managers gain reputation and career benefits in the market – by outperformance or by being as good as the benchmark only – and how much they risk in case they underperform their benchmark. Being directly asked whether herding benefits career (statement [1]), our respondents from all markets show mean values above three, i.e. they disagree on average – independent from their degree of trend following. Nevertheless, we find indications of individual rationality in herd behavior: In Thailand and Germany, except for those who indicate highest herding degree (answering category 1), we reveal that the more professionals indicate to herd, the more they believe in the career benefits of herding. In Russia, this relation is not that obvious, but those 15% of the sample who completely agree to herd, ascribe comparatively highest importance to herding's career benefits compared to other answering categories.

For the role of *relative performance for remuneration* (statement [2]), in Russia we find the relevance of relative performance to remarkably increase the more asset managers agree to be trend followers. From the compensational perspective, a strong benchmark orientation could thus indicate a conservative, but rational response to incentives. For Thai and German asset managers, the link between trend following and the importance of relative performance is less evident. However, those Thai asset managers who completely agree to be trend followers also assign highest relevance to relative performance compared to both, the rest of the Thai but also the whole sample (mean of 1.0). In the German sample, relative performance slightly gains relevance along herding categories 4 to 1. Interestingly, also those German asset managers who reject trend following (answering categories 5 and 6) judge their relative performance to be of high importance for them as well. These findings point towards a question raised by Lütje (2009): Do asset managers aim to be only as good as the benchmark, which would be in line with "hiding in the herd", or do they aspire to be better by deviating and outperforming others? The latter assumption could explain our results in the German sample.

The third explanation of herd behavior is given by *information cascades*. While we do not know which information signals individual market players receive in the different markets, we are able to directly ask them to assess relevant information categories used for investment decision making. In particular, we are interested in which relevance our surveyed asset managers assign to fundamental information, dependent on their degree of herd behavior. Fundamental facts may not only be assumed as least biased information type – even in an intransparent market environment. Their dominant use by important market players also supports a less psychologically biased price formation in the market. This in turn might prevent, or at least mediate, "blind" herd behavior. Asset managers' relevance of fundamentals as information source is also shown in Figure 5.1 (statement [3]). For German professionals, observations point towards less fundamentally driven behavior of herding asset managers: We find a higher trend following to be accompanied by lower relevance of fundamental information use and vice versa. In Russia and especially Thailand, the pattern is different. The following observation could be understood as a positive signal towards market efficiency and the role of asset managers for the latter in less transparent emerging markets: Although fundamentals are of high relevance in all three markets, their level of importance is highest in the emerging Thailand – for each degree of herding (means of 1.3 for answering category 1 and 1.2 for category 6). Also in the emerging Russia, highest agreement to follow the trend is accompanied by high relevance assigned to fundamentals (mean of 2.0), which is remarkably higher compared to the mean of 3.2 in Germany.

Figure 5.1: Herd behavior and its motives [(a)]

Please assess the following statements / source of information used in making investment decisions:

[1] "Following the herd benefits the asset manager's career." (Career benefit)

[2] "If you receive a performance-based remuneration, which criteria deter mine the size of that bonus?" (Relevance of relative performance)

[3] "Fundamental facts about the company / market." (Relevance of fundamentals)

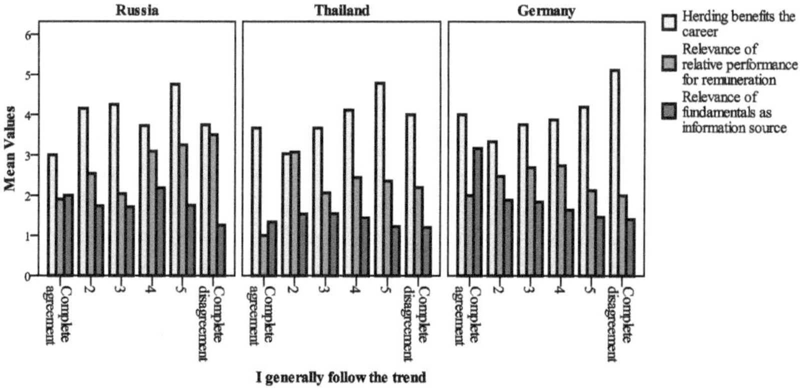

(a) For each statement, there are six answering categories, ranging from "complete agreement" / "highest relevance" (coded as 1) to "complete disagreement" / "no relevance" (6). Thus, a mean of 3.5 or less indicates rather approval to the statement.

Before jumping to conclusions, we bring herd behavior into a multivariate framework that allows us to control for interdependencies between the different motives of herd behavior as well as for risk behavior and personal characteristics. *Table 5.6* shows our findings from pooled ordered PROBIT regressions.

The results in the first regression indicate that, on the sample's average, a higher degree of herding is significantly linked to the belief in a career benefit, and indeed lower relevance of fundamental information. In order to control for possible formal restrictions, which individual asset managers might face due to their funds' strategies, we additionally include the amount asset managers attributed to momentum strategy in an extra control question. We reveal a complementary positive and significant impact of the latter on herd behavior.[75]

75 As we do not know how causality runs among trend following and momentum strategy, we ran the same regression with and without the momentum variable. In both cases, si-

Table 5.6: Herd behavior in a multivariate framework

[1] Common motives for herd behavior, [2] including emerging market variables, [3] and the influence of controlled risk-related variables	Ordered PROBIT regressions of herd behavior [(a)]					
	[1]		*[2]*		*[3]*	
Career benefit	**0.150*****	**(0.000)**	**0.156*****	**(0.000)**	**0.140*****	**(0.000)**
Relevance of relative performance	0.028	(0.160)	0.026	(0.197)	**0.041****	**(0.048)**
Relevance of fundamental information	**-0.186*****	**(0.001)**	**-0.206*****	**(0.000)**	**-0.214*****	**(0.000)**
Momentum strategy	**0.017*****	**(0.000)**	**0.017*****	**(0.000)**	**0.019*****	**(0.000)**
Country dummy RUS			**0.714*****	**(0.000)**	**0.635*****	**(0.000)**
Country dummy TH			**0.450*****	**(0.000)**	**0.219***	**(0.091)**
Female					-0.037	(0.491)
Experience					-0.020	(0.488)
Risk aversion					**0.141*****	**(0.005)**
Loss aversion					**0.158*****	**(0.000)**
Disposition effect					**0.074***	**(0.057)**
Number of included observations	453		453		453	
Log likelihood	-698.37		-681.49		-662.14	
LR statistics	86.23		119.98		158.69	
(Pseudo)-R^2	0.06		0.08		0.11	

(a) The table gives the coefficients of the respective ordered PROBIT regression with p-values in parentheses.

Stars refer to level of significance: * 10%, ** 5%, *** 1%

Furthermore, significant country-dummy variables for Russia and Thailand in the second regression underline a strong emerging markets effect in our sample. When controlling for personal characteristics and risk behavior in a third regression, we additionally find higher relevance of relative performance to add up to significant herding motives. Furthermore, and even more important,

gnificant findings for all the other variables as described in the following remain the same.

herd behavior is significantly linked to higher risk aversion, higher loss aversion, and a higher disposition effect.[76]

Summing up, our results highlight the strong influence of risk propensity for asset managers' herd behavior: Confirming compensation related aspects, assumed career benefits and less fundamentally driven information reliance to matter, we find particularly more risk averse and loss sensitive professionals to follow the herd. This finding gives strong support to the above mentioned real "fear" of falling out of the herd (cf. Graham, 1999), and the found evidence on risk propensity to be (mostly) lower among professionals from the two surveyed emerging markets. Thus, at least from the individual perspective, rationality in trend following cannot be denied – neither in Germany nor in Russia and Thailand.

Next, we will shed light on another behavioral bias, which may also be linked to asset managers' risk propensity. Again, we take a closer look at other influencing factors as well.

5.6 Home bias

Although global diversification opportunities have constantly increased over the last decades, it is well documented that to some extent investors still neglect the international capital market theory in this respect and miss chances to increase their risk-adjusted returns: They underweight foreign assets in their portfolios and allocate over-proportionately high shares to home assets instead. This phenomenon, widely known as 'home bias', has been related to several factors which French and Poterba (1991) divide into two categories: Institutional barriers and investor behavior.

While a home biased asset allocation was initially attributed to *governmental restrictions* and high transactions costs (cf. e.g. Stulz, 1981), strong advances in global financial integration have softened this argument (cf. e.g. Tesar and Werner, 1995, Ahearne et al., 2004). In its place, indirect barriers such as information asymmetries have received both broad research attention and empirical support to explain the home bias puzzle (cf. e.g. Gehrig, 1993, Coval and Moskowitz, 1999, Edison and Warnock, 2004). Related to the formerly described emerging markets' investment environment, the question of whether there is an information advantage either for foreign or domestic

76 Above findings from the third regression also widely hold when controlling for the set of risk variables in Germany and Thailand in particular (results are not explicitly displayed here).

investors remains controversial: While support in favor of domestic investors is found by Choe et al. (1999) in Korea and Dvorak (2005) in Indonesia, Seasholes (2004) finds little evidence of information disadvantages for foreign investors in Taiwan. By contrast, he detects foreign investors to outperform in certain stock types.

The behavioral perspective argues with investors' sentiments, which favor the domestic market, to explain the home bias. Such sentiments are e.g. the *return optimism* (cf. e.g. French and Poterba, 1991, Strong and Xu, 2003) or the *perceived higher competence* (cf. e.g. Kilka and Weber, 2000 as well as Graham et al., 2009, though with contrary findings) for domestic securities compared to foreign ones. Furthermore, studies on the role of *regional proximity* (cf. e.g. Coval and Moskowitz, 1999) and perceived *familiarity* (cf. e.g. Huberman, 2001) reveal these two factors to matter as well. Lütje and Menkhoff (2007), who provide survey evidence on German equity managers' home bias, analyze its different determinants and show them holding simultaneously in a multivariate framework.

Similar to our analysis of herd behavior, we first test the existence of a home-biased asset allocation. We therefore asked our surveyed asset managers to reveal their preferred international asset allocation, despite any fund restrictions. Highlighting the latter is important, as foreign investment restrictions are particularly limiting in Russia and Thailand (see Section 5.2).

According to the international capital market theory, the share of domestic assets in an investor's portfolio should equal the proportion of her domestic market's capitalization to the world market capitalization. Thus, according to the MSCI All Country World Index 2009, domestic assets in Russian portfolios should amount to a share of 0.7%, those in Thailand – to 0.2%, and those in Germany – to 3.2%.[77] *Figure 5.2* reveals our findings in regards to the surveyed asset managers' preferred allocation.

77 Data referring to September 2009 are given by MSCI Barra. In comparison, the United States account for 42%, Europe in total – for 27%, and Japan represents another 9% of world market capitalization.

Figure 5.2: Evidence on the home bias

Apart from any fund's restriction, please allocate an amount of 10 million USD / 500 million Baht / 10 million EUR to invest in the following regions (adding up to 100). Respective regions are given in [3].

[1] Histogram of preferred allocation to home market

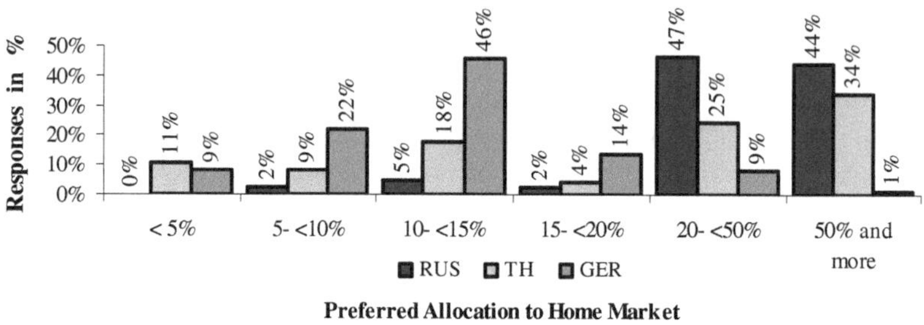

The histogram [1] in Figure 5.2 shows that only 11% of the Thai and 9% of the German asset managers prefer to allocate less than 5% of their portfolio to their respective home market. Those managers would thus, if at all, show a very limited home bias. However, in Russia, nobody would invest less than 5% of his portfolio to the Russian market. In contrast, the biggest group (46%) of German asset managers reveals a certain degree of home bias by allocating between 10% and 15% to the home market. Furthermore, we find the second-biggest fraction of Russian (44%) and the biggest fraction of Thai (34%) asset managers even among those, who would still allocate more than 50% to their home market.

Considering average values of the preferred domestic allocation relative to other markets in Figure 5.2 [2], our findings are threefold. First, in the Thai sample, Asia as a whole dominates. Even those asset managers that prefer less than 10% allocation to the domestic market reveal preferred allocation shares of around 50% to Asia in total. Hence, they show at least a strong *regional bias*, probably driven by geographic and cultural proximity. Among the three big developed markets, only Japan constantly receives a reasonable allocation share, when relying on the MSCI All Country World Index, while North America and Europe are clearly underrepresented.

[2] Preferred allocation to home market relative to other markets

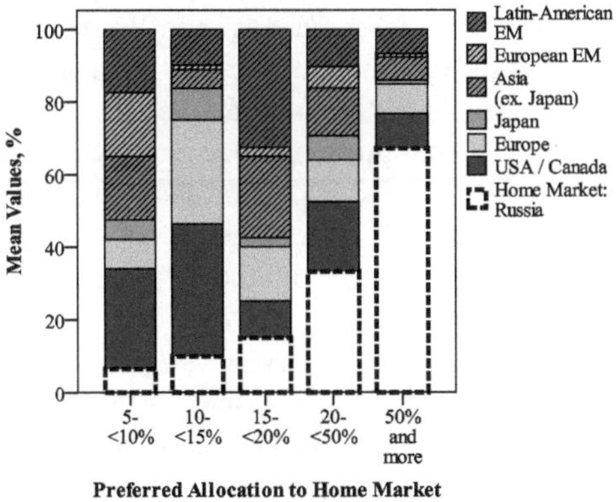

[3] Regions

Russia	*Mean*
Home market	46.0%
USA and Canada	15.7%
Europe	10.8%
Japan	4.2%
Asia (ex. Japan)	10.0%
Other European Emerging Markets	3.7%
Latin-American Emerging Markets	9.5%

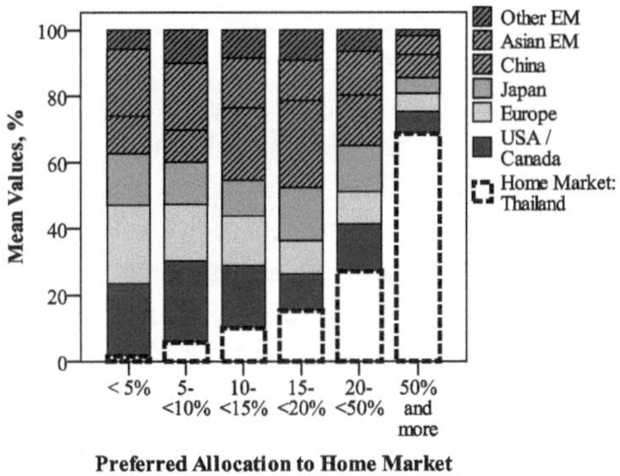

Thailand	
Home market	32.4%
USA and Canada	14.6%
Europe	11.6%
Japan	10.3%
China	13.2%
Asian Emerging Markets	12.4%
Other Emerging Markets	5.5%

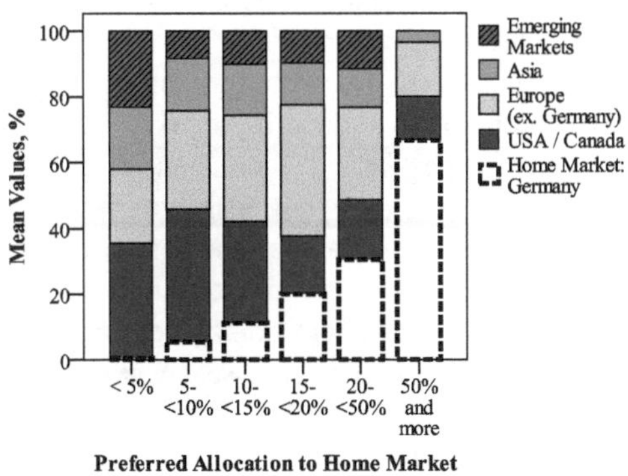

Germany	
Home market	12.5%
USA and Canada	30.3%
Europe (ex. Germany)	31.7%
Asia	14.9%
Emerging Markets	10.9%

Second, *least home-biased* German asset managers (those who would allocate less than 10% to the home market) are also *least biased in regards to other regions* – appropriately considering USA/Canada and Europe, and allocating a surprisingly high proportion to Asia and global emerging markets. A similar finding occurs in the Russian sample for a home market share of less than 15%. However, the preference for regional proximity becomes evident also in the German sample: With an increasing preferred allocation share to the home market, particularly North America loses weight, whereas the allocation share to Europe steadily grows and remains relatively high in the two most biased subgroups.

Third, it is interesting to learn about the perceived *attractiveness of emerging markets*. Least home-biased asset managers in markets would allocate the highest proportion to emerging markets (20% in Germany, almost 40% including China in Thailand, and even 50% in Russia). Shares of at least 30% in Thailand, and 10% in Germany, remain stable even with increasing home biased allocation, and only German managers with over 50% domestic allocation do not consider emerging markets any more.

Overall, also regarding the mean allocation shares in Figure 5.2 [3], the allocation shares to emerging markets are higher in our two emerging market samples compared to Germany. Interestingly, differences appear between the Russian and Thai preferences for diverse emerging markets regions. Whereas, as already mentioned, Thai asset managers rather focus on Asian emerging markets (including China) than on other emerging markets, Russian managers particularly favor Latin-American emerging markets (which would fall into the answering category "other emerging markets" in Thailand), besides the Asian ones. This implicates that, in contrast to their Thai peers, geographic and cultural proximity seems not to be decisive for investment decisions of Russian asset managers. An almost negligible share allocated to other nearby European emerging markets is in line with this interpretation.

In the following, we are interested to know which motives – besides possibly remaining institutional barriers in the two emerging markets – drive the home bias. Might informational advantages and (other than institutional) barriers, or behavioral explanations, such as return optimism contribute to its understanding? Therefore, we asked the asset managers whether they possess information advantages compared to foreign investors. In addition, we consider the relevance they attribute to fundamental facts about companies and market. Moreover, in Thailand and Germany, we also requested asset managers' long-term expectations for stock and bond market yields in both, their home market and the U.S. market as reference. Results are shown in *Figure 5.3*.

Figure 5.3: Different motives for home bias [(a)]

Home bias and its motives	Please assess the following statements regarding your investment behavior and the sources of information used in making investment decisions: [1] "As a domestic asset manager I benefit from better information on domestic securities compared to market players overseas." [2] "[I use] Fundamental facts about the company / market." [3] "What are your long-term expectations for the next 10 years? We would like to ask you to estimate the respective development within the next 10 years for the… - Stock market: average stock yield per year (in percent), - Bond market: average bond yield per year (in percent)."

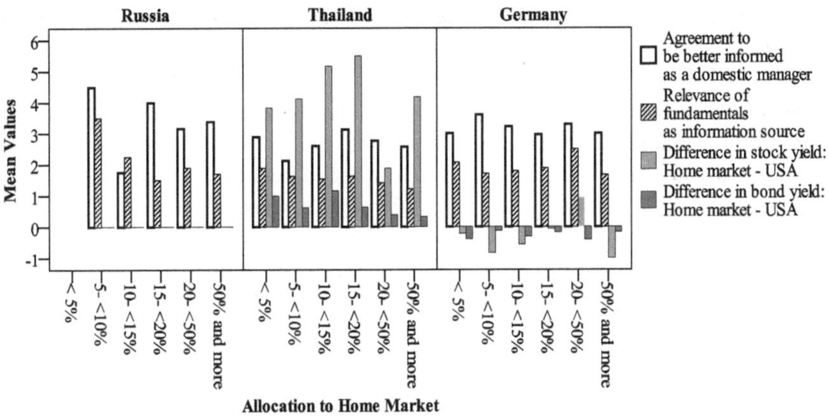

(a) Mean values for categorical responses range from "complete agreement"/ "highest relevance" (=1) to "complete disagreement" / "no relevance" (=6). Thus, a mean of 3.5 or less indicates rather approval to / high relevance of the statement. Stock and bond yield differences are given on a numerical scale and are only available for Thailand and Germany.

While overall findings for Russian and German asset managers do not reveal obvious relations, patterns for Thailand are more evident. To start with the agreement *to be better informed* as domestic manager, we find it to be highest for the two most home-biased groups in the Russian sample. Also in Thailand, the belief to possess domestic information advantages increases for a home allocation between 15% and 50%. Nevertheless, a clear pattern for this statement is missing in all samples. However, when taking the *relevance of fundamentals* into account, we observe the consistently positive coherence between a higher preferred home investment share and higher indicated relevance of fundamental facts in the Thai and, to some degree, also in the Russian sample. *Return expectations* offer a more convincing finding. Particularly regarding differences in stock yield expectations, we find a positive trend: The more asset managers expect their home market yields to increase compared to those in the U.S., the more they prefer to invest in their home market. In Thailand, this applies for home allocation shares up to 20% (positive differences). In Germany – even though yield differences between the German and the U.S. markets are negative in all subgroups – an increase in the home bias is accompanied by rising yield expectations for home stocks relative to the US market (as can be seen between 5% and 50%).

Findings from the multivariate framework, i.e. censored TOBIT regressions, again controlled for personal characteristics and risk variables, are shown in *Table 5.7.*

First, a higher preferred home allocation share is significantly linked to *higher expected stock yields in the home market*, as detected in the pooled sample of Thailand and Germany. As the data on stock and bond market yields is not available for the Russian sample, further regressions do not include these former variables. Among the two remaining motives for home-biased allocation, the *relevance of fundamental information* turns out to be significant. Second, compared to Germany (constant), the *emerging market effect* on the mean home allocation share is significant for both, Russia and Thailand, but comparably highest for Russia. Personal characteristics and risk variables brought into the regression reveal, third, a highly significant *gender* influence as well as significant positive linkages between home bias and *disposition effect*, but negative ones between home bias and *loss aversion.*

As the emerging market dummies remain significant, next, we test whether the revealed effects on the home allocation share differ between the two emerging markets and Germany, respectively. For this purpose, we include eight interaction terms in the fourth regression. Theses interaction terms are defined as respective products of the emerging market dummies (dummy RUS and dummy TH) with the four significant variables from regression three, i.e. relevance of fundamental information, gender, loss aversion, and disposition effect. Having coded the German sample "0" in both emerging market dummies, respectively, we may think of the German sample as the "reference group" against which we will compare the two emerging markets Russia and Thailand. The coefficient for an interaction term (dummy*independent variable) measures the differential effect of the independent variable between the two groups defined in the dummy variable.

Table 5.7: Home bias in a multivariate framework

[1] Common motives for home-biased allocation, [2] including emerging market variables, [3]-[4] and the influence of controlled risk-related variables	Censored TOBIT regressions of home investment share [(a)]				
	[1] only TH/GER[(b)]	*[1] whole sample*	*[2]*	*[3]*	*[4]*
Constant	**19.760*** (0.000)**	**26.106*** (0.000)**	**11.783*** (0.000)**	**12.002** (0.044)**	**22.771*** (0.000)**
Better informed as domestic manager	1.070 (0.159)	-0.525 (0.532)	-0.828 (0.235)	-1.012 (0.144)	-0.886 (0.198)
Relevance of fundamental information	0.862 (0.427)	**2.451* (0.054)**	**1.800* (0.086)**	**1.935* (0.060)**	0.217 (0.865)
Stock market yield Home-USA	**0.785*** (0.009)**				
Bond market yield Home-USA	-0.708 (0.520)				
Country dummy RUS			**34.779*** (0.000)**	**35.361*** (0.000)**	
Country dummy TH			**20.616*** (0.000)**	**17.315*** (0.000)**	
Female				**3.232*** (0.003)**	0.111 (0.936)
Experience				0.624 (0.265)	0.649 (0.240)
Risk aversion				1.377 (0.138)	0.766 (0.405)
Loss aversion				**-1.389* (0.097)**	1.156 (0.293)
Disposition effect				**1.877** (0.012)**	**1.815* (0.064)**
Relevance of fundamental information RUS [(c)]					1.798 (0.426)
Relevance of fundamental information TH [(c)]					**8.702*** (0.001)**
Female RUS [(c)]					**9.319** (0.019)**
Female TH [(c)]					**7.446*** (0.000)**

Loss aversion RUS [(c)]					**-4.812**** **(0.014)**
Loss aversion TH [(c)]					**-5.162***** **(0.002)**
Disposition effect RUS [(c)]					-1.403 (0.444)
Disposition effect TH [(c)]					1.017 (0.537)
Number of included observations	261	444	444	444	444
Log likelihood	-1048.62	-1969.10	-1884.145	-1874.42	-1867.20
R^2 (adjusted)	0.04	-0.002	0.32	0.35	0.36

(a) The table gives the coefficients of the censored TOBIT regression with p-values in parentheses.

(b) The data on stock and bond market yields is only available for the Thai and German samples.

(c) These variables are given as interaction terms, i.e. the respective products of dummy RUS and dummy TH with the significant variables from the regression [3], i.e. relevance of fundamental information, female, loss aversion, and disposition effect.

Stars refer to level of significance: * 10%, ** 5%, *** 1%

Thus, regression [4] shows that higher *disposition effect* significantly contributes to a higher home bias in the whole sample (an effect that does not significantly differ across our three markets, as the coefficients for the interaction terms are not significant). Emerging market effects appear in the following: Particularly *female* asset managers as well as those displaying lower *loss aversion* in Russia and Thailand allocate an even higher investment share to their home markets than do their average sample counterparts in regression [3]. Besides, high relevance assigned to *fundamental information* significantly strengthens only Thai asset managers' preference for their home market, compared to Germany.

So far, academic research is still scarce on linkages between home bias and disposition effect as well as home bias and gender. Karlsson and Nordén (2007), for example, analyze the existence of home bias in mutual fund portfolios that are part of the Swedish pension plan. Looking at the individual investor and controlling for age, individual wealth and the amount invested in analyzed pension funds, they do, however, find older male investors slightly more inclined to invest domestically than females. In contrast, Graham et al. (2009) provide evidence that is in line with our findings. Analyzing data from the UBS/Gallup Investor Survey, they link perceived investor competence to trading activity and home bias. Similar to Barber and Odean (2001) who find particular young male investors to trade too much, Graham et al. (2009) detect male investors to be more likely to perceive themselves as competent and thus showing a higher trading activity. Besides, by feeling more competent also about foreign investments, male investors are less likely to exhibit a home-biased asset allocation than their female counterparts. Krause et al. (2006) close the circle by their analysis of Chinese stock and fund accounts. Finding active traders to be less prone to display a disposition effect, they do not detect any statistically significant gender difference in their multivariate framework regarding the disposition effect. Further research to reach a more coherent framework linking observed behavioral biases as well as the role of personal characteristics in mutual fund investments, such as gender differences, is clearly needed.

5.7 Conclusion and outlook

This study offers new insights into asset managers' behavior by presenting comparative survey evidence from two emerging markets, Russia and Thailand, as well as a developed one, Germany. This implies a comparison of professionals' acting in diverging investment environments concerning market transparency, information efficiency, institutional development, and regulatory restrictions. Particularly, we test the hypothesis that fund managers from emerging markets behave more biased than do their peers from developed markets.

Indeed, we find the answers of fund managers from Russia and Thailand to significantly deviate (in the same direction) from their German peers. This indicates fund managers from emerging markets to be more biased regarding loss aversion and disposition effect as well as the two well-known financial market phenomena, herding and home bias. We analyze the motives for the latter in more detail.

Starting with trend following, by which we grasp the degree of fund managers' herd behavior, we find evidence for two major aspects. First, the imitation of others market players' decisions seems to be linked to both, reputation concerns and the importance of relative performance for compensation. Those managers who herd seem to be afraid of falling out of the herd. They thus perceive staying within the herding group as career protection or even career benefit. This finding is robust when controlling for personal and risk variables. In this respect, we detect risk and loss aversion as well as the disposition effect to positively influence fund managers' herd behavior. Thus, from an individual perspective, revealed herding can be considered as rational – at least to some degree – in both, emerging and developed market environments. Second, the evidence for information based herding is mixed. We find that herd behavior is significantly linked to lower importance of fundamentals in general. However, some hints for coexistence of herding and higher fundamental orientation are detected in one emerging market.

So far, our results may possibly contribute to concerns about the impact of obviously risk-driven behavioral biases on market prices and efficiency – especially in emerging markets. The danger of uninformed investment behavior to reinforce market trends and crises has been widely described by e.g. Hirshleifer (2001), Chari and Kehoe (2003), or Shiller (2003). Besides, Coval and Shumway (2005) find evidence for loss averse traders to cause short-term price impacts. However, good news for improvements of market efficiency comes from our surveyed asset managers in Russia and Thailand: Trend followers in emerging markets assign more importance to fundamental information than do their German counterparts. Besides, we can only speculate how much their risk behavior has been influenced by e.g. experiences from the Asian or Russian financial crises, which made both professionals and private investors painfully aware of possible downside risks in the market.

From our home bias analysis, we want to highlight three findings. First, a surprisingly high influence of institutional barriers can be named responsible for extraordinary high home market investment share preferred by the average asset manager from an emerging market. Second, we disclose a striking preference for regional proximity and thus familiarity especially in Thailand. These motives are comparatively weaker in Germany. However, they obviously lose relevance in Russia. Moreover, our results confirm the significance of return optimism (for the joint sample Thailand and Germany). Third, professionals' risk biases also seem to influence a home-biased asset allocation. The latter goes along with a higher disposition effect in the whole sample, but is negatively affected by loss aversion, which is more pronounced in the two emerging markets.

Our illustrations on preferred allocation have shown that mostly in Thailand, but also in Germany, regional relatedness is observable – almost independently from the allocation share to the domestic market. This result reflects general preferences for cultural, lingual, and geographic proximity, and thus supports the literature identifying preference for conformity as one important motive for the home bias. Higher return expectations for the home market provide another behavioral explanation for the home bias in our analysis – either driven by optimism or even by realism. Detecting further coherences with risk-related biases and sharpening knowledge about gender influences remains open for future research on mutual fund managers' behavior.

For policy makers and investment professionals, our study impressively demonstrates the predominant influence of existing foreign investment restrictions in the two emerging markets: Even in a simulated unrestricted framework, more than one third of the surveyed asset managers from Russia and Thailand reveal preferred domestic allocation shares of more than 50%. Therefore, preparing and promoting a reasonable exploitation of the advantages from international diversification will be an important task to face for asset managers and regulators in emerging markets. However, considering that asset managers act on behalf of their clients, it will be interesting to observe the development in customers' demand in the future. So far, individual investors in emerging markets, similarly to professionals, are still confronted with strong regulatory restrictions regarding investment opportunities (abroad). Nevertheless, steady fund inflows to the still limited number of offered internationally-diversified funds point towards customers' interest not only for domestic investments, but also for regional and international allocation opportunities.

6. Exchange rate exposure of Central and Eastern European exporting firms[78]

6.1 Introduction

The exchange rate exposure of firms, i.e. the sensitivity of firms' stock returns to fluctuations in foreign exchange rates, has been widely discussed since the end of the Bretton Woods system. Theoretical research, such as e.g. by Bodnar et al. (2002), underpins its importance for a firm's value by identifying various channels through which exchange rate shocks are assumed to affect a firm's profitability. Hence, from this perspective, a firm's foreign exchange exposure should be thought relevant not only for risk management decisions of corporate managers, but also for international investors who seek to hedge their portfolio. Finally, it should also be of interest for policy makers who have to decide about the appropriate exchange rate arrangement for a country. However, the empirical evidence on the theoretically suggested relevance of the exposure is mixed at best (Bodnar and Wong, 2003, He and Ng, 1998, see also Muller and Verschoor, 2006a).

Our study sheds light on the exchange rate exposure of exporting firms in the four transition markets Russia, Czech Republic, Hungary, and Poland. Transition markets have been least focused for this analysis so far. Most of empirical work is on Western industrialized economies (see e.g. Chamberlain et al., 1997, Glaum, 2000), where the exposure is found to be rather modest. However, empirical results suggest that exchange rate exposure seems to be higher in emerging economies: Kiymaz (2003) for example finds that the comparatively high share of 50% of Turkish firms is exposed to foreign exchange risk. Parsley and Popper (2006) find a substantial share of South East Asian firms to be exposed. Choe and Cook (2008) analyze 900 emerging market firms, but excluding transition economies, and find exposures of mixed sign. Entorf et al. (2005), who include the transition economies Czech Republic, Hungary and Poland to their sample of 27 countries, provide a similar result. The first study solely on Eastern European firms is presented by Muller and Verschoor (2007). They find a significant and on average positively signed exchange rate exposure for 19% of Czech, Hungarian and Polish multinational

78 I would like to thank my co-author Michael Frömmel. Helpful comments by Lukas Menkhoff, Vadim S. Kufenko and Nora Srzentic are gratefully acknowledged. We thank Fabian Bätje, Ekaterina Gracheva, and Marie Theres Holzhausen for their research assistance.

firms. Besides, they report a relation of the exchange rate exposure with firm size and trade openness. However, they only measure the exposure to fluctuations versus the US Dollar.

The number of studies on Central and Eastern European Countries (CEEC) is surprisingly small, as five factors make them an interesting region for analyzing exchange rate exposure. First, most of the countries show an extremely high degree of international trade integration and, thus, form examples of highly open economies. This mainly applies to the new member states of the European Union, but also for Russia, as one of the world's largest exporters of oil and gas. Second, firms in CEEC have less access to financial instruments for hedging their foreign exchange risk. This is due to the comparatively less liquid financial and particularly the foreign exchange market. This lack of *financial* hedging instruments may also result in a currency mismatch and is seen as one of the main reasons for the well-known "fear of floating"-phenomenon. These first factors, the high degree of trade integration on the one hand, and the lack of hedging opportunities at the same time, mean that firms in CEEC are more vulnerable to shocks from the foreign exchange markets. Third, compared to industrialized countries, firms in CEEC are less international. Since the CEEC have been transformed into market oriented economic systems only since the 1990's, their firms had less opportunities to expand internationally and thus diversify their economic activities over different currency areas. Fourth, and from a European perspective most important, the CEEC as well as Russia have become important trade partners in the European Union. Thus, the analysis of their exposure to the Euro, besides the one to the US Dollar, is of high relevance as well. Fifth and finally, since the history of CEEC covers various different exchange rate arrangements, including comparatively rigid horizontal and crawling pegs, managed and free floats, they allow studying possible effects of the exchange rate system on exchange rate exposure of firms. For all of these reasons, we expect the exposure of the Eastern European firms to be more pronounced than that found in Western industrialized economies.

Therefore, we contribute to the literature by, first, providing evidence on the exchange rate exposure of exporting firms in the transition markets Czech Republic, Hungary, Poland, and Russia, which is surprisingly rare so far. Second, we address the ambiguity of findings in the literature by a different approach: Thinking of various possible exposure channels – e.g. trough competitiveness, foreign denominated debt, or portfolio investments – we assume that the relevance of these channels and thus the direction of exposure may vary in single markets. Hence, we do not pool all countries in just one joint sample, but regard the CEEC-3 and Russia separately. This split should avoid a canceling-out of opposite exposure directions, if there were any. It can be justified by similar export structures within the CEEC-3, which clearly differ from the Russian one. Third, in addition to the US Dollar, we also analyze the exposure to the Euro, which has been neglected in the literature for Eastern Europe so far. Forth, since most CEEC started with comparatively tight pegs, before they proceeded to more flexible exchange rate arrangements, the question arises whether the exchange rate regime affects the foreign exchange risk exposure of firms. Our chosen period from September 1995 to April 2009 allows to examine this.

The evidence rather favors our approach. First, we find over 80% of exporting firms in our sample to be significantly exposed to daily exchange rate movements in both, Russia and the CEEC-3. This exposure is clearly higher than those reported in the literature so far (e.g. 20% in Dominguez and Tesar (2006) for eight (non-US) industrialized and emerging markets; 19% in Muller and Verschoor (2007) for Czech Republic, Hungary, and Poland). Second, in Russia and the CEEC-3, the exposures to the US Dollar and Euro indeed have different magnitudes and opposed directions – a significant finding, not yet documented in the literature. In detail, the exposure of exporting firms' stock returns to the US Dollar is considerable and negative in Russia, but only slight and positive in the CEEC-3. In contrast, the exposure to the Euro is slightly negative and not significant in Russia, but considerable and positive in the CEEC-3.[79] Finally, the exposure seems not to be substantially influenced by fixed exchange rate regimes.

Several implications can be derived from our results. If we had analyzed both, the CEEC-3 and Russia, in one joint sample, the revealed opposite exposures would (at least partly) cancel each other out, thus producing a rather modest average exposure similar to those documented in other studies. Furthermore, our findings confirm the convincing intuition for the significant dependence of the CEEC-3 on the Euro rate and also support the expectation for a differing importance of exposure transmission channels in single countries: Whereas the competitiveness channel appears to dominate in Russia, in the CEEC-3, this is more likely the foreign debt channel.

The remainder of the paper is organized as follows. The subsequent Section 6.2 reviews the theoretical rationale behind exchange rate exposure. Section 6.3 and Section 6.4 introduce our dataset and methodology. Our empirical results are described in Section 6.5, while Section 6.6 summarizes and concludes.

---

79 A negative (positive) exposure means that a depreciation of the domestic currency goes along with an increase (decrease) of a firm's share price.

6.2 The FX Exposure of Firms

There are several potential reasons why a firm's value may be exposed to movements on the foreign exchange market. First, an appreciation of the domestic currency may erode a firm's *competitiveness* on international markets, since the revenues of the firm get smaller. Besides this competitive exposure, a depreciation of the domestic currency increases the revenues and, thus, the exporting firm's benefits. The effect does of course reverse for importing firms, as the price for their imports in local currency rise. Even if a company is purely domestic, i.e., it does not export nor import at all, it might be affected through the channel of competitiveness, as an appreciation of the domestic currency may support foreign competitors in the domestic market. Furthermore, exporting firms are often supposed to hold foreign assets related to their foreign business. The value of foreign assets decreases (increases) with an appreciation (depreciation) of the domestic currencies. Based on the effects of competition and foreign assets, firms are sometimes classified as importing, exporting or domestic, i.e. firms with high foreign assets are treated as exporting firms.

Second, domestic firms with net *foreign denominated debt* will gain (lose) with an appreciating (depreciating) domestic currency[80]. This was a problem in CEEC particularly during the first years of transition, as the underdeveloped financial markets forced firms to borrow abroad, whereas foreign lenders were not willing to lend in the currency of the transition economy, which led to a currency mismatch (see Eichengreen et al., 2003, the "original sin"). Obviously the effect of foreign denominated debt is unrelated with the firm's role as an exporter or importer, but solely depends on the financing structure of the company.

Finally, share prices and currency fluctuations may be connected via *capital flows* due to *portfolio investments*. If foreign investors buy domestic stocks they might move both, the exchange rate and the stock price. Although this implies a co-movement of the domestic currency and the stock price – rather than what is traditionally understood as the foreign exchange exposure – this relation may be found in empirical testing. Similarly to foreign debt, portfolio investments are of particular importance for CEEC, which have been exposed to substantial amounts of capital inflows (or outflows) during the last decades, making them more similar to other emerging economies than to industrialized developed countries.

80 This is part of the translation exposure (Muller and Verschoor 2006a). There may of course also be the case of foreign assets, which is less relevant for transition economies. Muller and Verschoor (2006a) furthermore refer to transaction and contractual exposure. Since their effect should be short-lived we do not consider them further.

Table 6.1: Relations between share prices and exchange rate

	Exporting firms	Importing firms	Domestic firms
Competitiveness channel	– [(a)]	+	(+) [(b)]
Foreign debt channel	+	+	+
Portfolio channel	+	+	+

(a) "– ": negative correlation between domestic currency and share prices. i.e. depreciation (appreciation) of the domestic currency goes along with an increase (decrease) of share prices.

(b) Potential and weaker indirect effect via foreign competitors on the domestic market.

Table 6.1 summarizes the respective effects on share prices. The case is obviously easier for importing and domestic firms, for which all channels point to the same direction. In contrast, the share prices of exporting firms may on the one hand benefit from a depreciation due to increased competitiveness, or they may suffer from the increased debt burden or from lower demand due to capital outflows that at the same time let the currency depreciate.

The ambiguous relations between exchange rate fluctuations and share prices also explain why empirical studies in most cases find a comparatively low foreign exchange exposure (for a survey see Muller and Verschoor, 2006a). The question of which effect is dominating is therefore an empirical one and does not even necessarily lead to the same result in each single country.

6.3 Data

This study considers the stock markets of Russia, Czech Republic, Hungary, and Poland (CEEC-3). Thereby, the focus is on daily returns of all stocks which have ever been included to the respective domestic stock index and which are available on DataStream. The use of daily data is common in the literature (see e.g. Chamberlain et al., 1997, Di Iorio and Faff, 2000, Glaum, 2000). As can be seen from *Table 6.2*, our sample includes 92 stocks (out of 133 stocks which have ever been in the index) from the stock index RTS in Russia, 12 (55) from the PX in the Czech Republic, 17 (18) from the BUX in Hungary, and 28 (49) from the WIG in Poland. Our sample covers the period from September 1st, 1995 – April 30th, 2009, and therefore nearly the whole transition period, except the most volatile phase in its earliest stage.

Table 6.2: Descriptive statistics

	All stocks [a]	Exporting (N)	Importing (N)	Domestic (N)
Russian Federation (RTS)	92 (133)	30	4	58
CEEC-3:	57 (122)	21	3	33
- Czech Republic(PX)	12 (55)	4	0	8
- Hungary (BUX)	17 (18)	6	0	11
- Poland (WIG)	28 (49)	11	3	14
Total number:	149 (255)	51	7	91

(a) Number (N) of stocks available in DataStream (number of all stocks ever been included in the index).

We assign each market's stocks to three portfolios, containing exporting, importing and domestic firms, respectively. A firm is defined as an "exporting" ("importing") one if the share of its revenues from export (import) sales to total sales exceeds 40%. If both shares are below 40%, a company is assigned to the portfolio "domestic". Overall, this classification results in 51 exporting firms, 7 importing firms and 91 domestic firms. Due to the small number of importing firms, we only focus on exporting and domestic stocks in further analysis. The *appendix* additionally gives a short description of exporting firms' activities as well as their engagement in export sales.

The three EU-markets Czech Republic, Hungary, and Poland are also jointly analyzed as a CEEC-3 group, since only a small number of stocks is available for a single country, in particular for the Czech Republic or Hungary. This grouping can be justified by the fact that the three countries turn out to provide quite similar results. Thus, we end up with two comparatively homogeneous groups: Russia with 30 exporting and 58 domestic, and the CEEC-3 with 21 exporting and 33 domestic firms' stocks (see Table 6.2).

To construct the effective exchange rates EUR/CEEC-3 and USD/CEEC-3, we use the IMF DOT (direction of trade) statistics data on the Czech, Hungarian and Polish exports to the Euro-Area-16 and the USA. The weight for the respective country's exchange rate is calculated as its respective share of export in the total CEEC-3 exports to the Euro-Area-16 and the USA.

This results in a rather equal weighting of the three exchange rates regarded:

$$\Delta EUR/CEEC\text{-}3 = 0.37 \cdot \Delta(EUR/CZK) + 0.28 \cdot \Delta(EUR/HUF) + 0.35 \cdot \Delta(EUR/PLZ)$$
$$\Delta USD/CEEC\text{-}3 = 0.32 \cdot \Delta(USD/CZK) + 0.36 \cdot \Delta(USD/HUF) + 0.32 \cdot \Delta(USD/PLZ)$$

6.4 Methodology

We measure exchange rate exposure by estimating the equation

$$r_{i,t} = \alpha_i + \beta_i \cdot r_{m,t} + \gamma_{i,€} \cdot \Delta e_€ + \gamma_{i,\$} \cdot \Delta e_\$ + \Sigma_{k=1..K} \delta_{i,k} \cdot D_{t,k} + \varepsilon_t \quad (1)$$

which is an extension of the commonly used approach by Adler and Dumas (1984) and Jorion (1990). In equation (1) $r_{i,t}$ is the return of a portfolio of stocks or a single share i on day t; $r_{m,t}$ is the return of a benchmark portfolio; $\Delta e_€$ and $\Delta e_\$$ are changes of the price of the domestic currency versus the Euro and the US Dollar, respectively[81]. Such bilateral rates have been used, for instance, by Williamson (2001) and Parsley and Popper (2006), while most existing studies rely on effective exchange rates. Although not incorporating it in one equation, Dominguez and Tesar (2006) also stress the different importance of currencies for the exposure. $D_{t,k}$ are appropriate dummies, i.e. for the introduction of the Euro (January 1, 1999) and for the accession to the European Union (January 1, 2004 for the CEEC-3). In addition, our regression also contains calendar dummies for January and December to account for a potential turn-of-the-year effect (see Reinganum, 1983).[82]

The benchmark portfolio differs from the market portfolio in two respects: First, in line with Pritamani et al. (2004), it only contains shares of domestic stocks. This is to avoid that it is affected by the exchange rate exposure of exporting firms under consideration here. Second, since one may also expect domestic firms to be exposed to exchange rate changes, a multicollinearity problem occurs. We therefore additionally orthogonalize the market return on exchange rate fluctuations by running a side regression of the portfolio of domestic stocks on exchange rate changes, as suggested by, e.g., He et al. (1996)

81 The use of the changes of the domestic currency against the US Dollar and the Euro in the same equation may potentially lead to multicollinearity problems, which make it difficult to distinguish the individual effects of the currencies. The reason is that multicollinearity, although it will not bias the estimates, increases the standard errors on the individual coefficient estimates. However, multicollinearity seems not to be a serious problem. The correlations between the exchange rate returns versus the US Dollar and Euro respectively are about 0.45. Both, Parsley and Popper (2006) and Williamson (2001), use a similar approach and find correlation that in some cases reach 80-90%. As in our analysis, they do not experience estimation problems in terms of inflated standard errors.

82 We also added dummies to account for potential day-of-the-week effects. The results however, are not significant nor do they improve the estimations. Therefore we do not report them, they are available from the authors on request.

or Kiymaz (2003)[83]. Our benchmark return therefore measures the market return that is not explained by currency fluctuations. Accordingly, the coefficients $\gamma_{i,€}$ and $\gamma_{i,\$}$ provide the residual exchange rate exposure of firm i (Muller and Verschoor, 2006a).

Since financial time series at daily frequency generally suffer from hetereoskedasticity and volatility clustering, we model the error term ε_t as a GJR-GARCH model (Glosten et al., 1993) that additionally allows for an asymmetric reaction of volatility to the sign of the previous return:

$$\varepsilon_t \sim N(0,\sigma_t^2) \quad \sigma_t^2 = \omega + \alpha \cdot \sigma_{t-1}^2 + \beta \cdot \varepsilon_{t-1}^2 + \gamma \cdot I_{>0}(\varepsilon_{t-1}) \tag{2}$$

where $I_{>0}(\cdot)$ is an indicator function that takes the value one, if the argument is positive and zero else. The estimates show that the use of a GARCH-type model is justified, the coefficients α and β, and in most cases also γ are significant and reflect both, conditional heteroskedasticity and asymmetry in the volatility process.

Equation (1) treats the exchange rate exposure as being constant over time. Since the choice of an exchange rate regime may also affect firms' exposure to currency risk, we additionally use dummy variables that reflect fixed exchange rate regimes and estimate interaction terms of these dummies with the exchange rate exposure coefficients. Equation (1) then evolves to:

$$\begin{aligned} r_{i,t} = {} & \alpha_i + \beta_i \cdot r_{m,t} + \gamma_{i,€} \cdot \Delta e_€ + \gamma_{i,\$} \cdot \Delta e_\$ + \Sigma_{k=1..K} \delta_{i,k} \cdot D_{t,k} + \\ & + \Sigma_{k=1..K}(\vartheta_{i,€} \cdot \Delta e_€ D_{t,k} + \vartheta_{i,\$} \cdot \Delta e_\$ D_{t,k}) + \varepsilon_t \end{aligned} \tag{3}$$

and differs from equation (1) by the interaction terms $\cdot \Delta e_€ D_{t,k,€}$ and $\cdot \Delta e_\$ D_{t,k\$}$, which shall capture a change in the foreign exchange risk exposure during times of fixed exchange rate regimes.

The dummies $D_{t,k,€}$ and $D_{t,k\$}$ take the value one, if the domestic currency is pegged to the € or \$ respectively, and zero else. In detail, these dummies indicate the following periods. Before passing over into a managed or a free float, in the Czech Republic, the exchange rate was pegged to a basket of Deutsche Mark and US Dollar until May 26, 1997; in Poland – to a basket including both, Deutsche Mark/EUR and US Dollar, until April 11, 2000; and in Hungary – to a basket of Deutsche Mark/EUR and US Dollar until December 31, 1999, and only to EUR since January 1st, 2000 until February 26, 2008. As

83 As a robustness check we also regressed the exchange rate changes on the benchmark portfolio, as also found in the literature (see Choi and Prasad 1995). This does, however, not substantially change the results.

the time of abandoning the fixed exchange rate regime differ, it is not possible to introduce one joint dummy variable for all the three CEEC markets here. In the Russian Federation, there are two regime switches observable in our sample. During the Russian crisis, the initial peg to the US Dollar was replaced by a floating exchange rate regime starting on September 2nd, 1998. However, since February 1st, 2005 the Ruble has been again pegged, this time to a bi-currency basket consisting of Euro and US Dollar.

6.5 Empirical Results

The estimation results for the portfolios are given in *Table 6.3.1* (portfolio of exporting firms) and *6.3.2* (benchmark portfolio) respectively. In all equations in Table 6.3.1 the relation with the benchmark portfolio is highly significant and of considerable size. In contrast, the impact of the remaining variables differs substantially. We find significant January and December effects for the CEEC-3, which are obviously mainly due to the Polish market. The introduction of the Euro in 1999 and the accession of the CEEC-3 to the European Union in 2004 only have a marginal (although in some cases significant) effect. Furthermore, we find a significant, but economically negligible effect of both variables on the Russian domestic portfolio (Table 6.3.2).

However, the coefficients on the exchange rate exposure show, first, a clear and significant pattern, and second, remarkable differences between Russia on the one and the CEEC3 on the other hand.

Both, the Russian and the Central European stocks show a significant relation with exchange rate changes. This applies to exporting firms and for Russia also to domestic firms. The effect is economically significant; the most pronounced coefficients are close to 0.4, meaning that a one per cent change in the exchange rate goes along with a change in the stock return by almost 0.4 per cent. This result is roughly in line with Chue and Cook (2008), who report an average (but positive) exposure of 0.4 using an effective exchange rate.

It turns out that stocks of exporting firms (Table 6.3.1) on the Russian market react strongly and significantly negatively to changes in the USD/RUB exchange rate, meaning that a depreciation of the Ruble leads ceteris paribus to increasing share prices. This is in line with the competitiveness channel, which means that foreign revenues of Russian exporters increase, if the Ruble depreciates.

Table 6.3.1: Portfolio results for exporting firms and exchange rate regimes

	Results for the mean equation of a GJR (1,1) regression [a]								
	Russia		*CEEC-3*	*Czech Republic*		*Hungary*		*Poland*	
		Regime			*Regime*		*Regime*		*Regime*
c	0.000 (0.307)	0.000 (0.295)	**0.001***** **(0.000)**	**-0.001***** **(0.000)**	**-0.001***** **(0.000)**	**0.001***** **(0.000)**	**0.001***** **(0.001)**	**0.001***** **(0.000)**	**0.001***** **(0.001)**
r_D	**0.469***** **(0.000)**	**0.473***** **(0.000)**	**0.710***** **(0.000)**	**0.578***** **(0.000)**	**0.556***** **(0.000)**	**0.454***** **(0.000)**	**0.453***** **(0.000)**	**0.454***** **(0.000)**	**0.449***** **(0.000)**
Δe€	-0.010 (0.507)	-0.005 (0.794)	**0.393***** **(0.000)**	0.017 (0.436)	0.006 (0.797)	**0.144***** **(0.000)**	**0.133***** **(0.000)**	**0.354***** **(0.000)**	**0.304***** **(0.000)**
Δe$	**-0.379***** **(0.000)**	**-0.389***** **(0.000)**	**0.065***** **(0.000)**	0.012 (0.449)	0.015 (0.329)	**-0.030***** **(0.002)**	**-0.026**** **(0.014)**	**0.071***** **(0.000)**	**0.094***** **(0.000)**
JAN	0.000 (0.804)	0.000 (0.805)	**0.001**** **(0.042)**	0.000 (0.295)	0.000 (0.169)	0.000 (0.845)	0.000 (0.835)	0.001 (0.331)	0.001 (0.288)
DEZ	0.000 (0.745)	0.000 (0.748)	**0.001***** **(0.001)**	0.000 (0.383)	0.000 (0.279)	0.000 (0.893)	0.000 (0.890)	**0.003***** **(0.000)**	**0.003***** **(0.000)**
Euro 1999	0.000 (0.672)	0.000 (0.710)	0.000 (0.182)	**0.001***** **(0.001)**	**0.001***** **(0.001)**	**0.000*** **(0.052)**	**0.000*** **(0.073)**	**-0.001**** **(0.023)**	**-0.001*** **(0.088)**
EU 2004	0.000 (0.324)	0.000 (0.319)	**0.000**** **(0.020)**	0.000 (0.956)	0.000 (0.944)	0.000 (0.242)	0.000 (0.240)	**-0.001**** **(0.045)**	**-0.001*** **(0.056)**
fix $\Delta e_€$		-0.004 (0.922)			0.101 (0.189)		0.012 (0.587)		**0.200***** **(0.000)**
fix $\Delta e_\$$		0.023 (0.499)			**0.521***** **(0.000)**		**-0.056*** **(0.073)**		**-0.182***** **(0.003)**
Adj. R^2	0.45	0.45	0.55	0.12	0.09	0.44	0.44	0.50	0.50
DW [b]	2.0	2.0	1.8	1.8	1.8	1.9	1.9	1.8	1.8

(a) The exchange rate is given in indirect quotation (foreign to domestic currency). Thus, a negative coefficient means that a depreciation (appreciation) of the domestic currency, or a decrease (increase) in the exchange rate, goes along with an increase (decrease) in share prices and vice versa. JAN, DEZ, Euro 1999, EU 2004 are the dummy variables as explained in Section 6.4. fix Δe€ and fix Δe$ are the interaction terms between exchange rate fluctuation and the exchange rate regime.

(b) Durbin Watson (DW) test.

Stars refer to level of significance: * 10%, ** 5%, *** 1%

This observation can be explained by the particular structure of the Russian exporting sector, which is characterized by a substantial share of oil and gas exporting firms, but also companies from the metals and mining sector. Since these products are to a large extent traded in US Dollar, while most of the expenses are paid in Ruble, a depreciation of the Ruble immediately increases the firm's profits. Accordingly, the reaction of Russian exporting firms to changes in the EUR/RUB rate is moderate and insignificant.

Exporting firms in the CEEC-3, i.e. Czech Republic, Hungary and Poland, show different behavior: In contrast to Russian exporting firms, their returns are mainly exposed to changes in the Euro exchange rate, and only to a small extent (albeit significantly) to changes in the US Dollar exchange rate. Furthermore, their currency risk exposure shows the opposite sign compared with the Russian exporting firms, i.e. an appreciation of the domestic currencies goes along with price increases of the exporting firms.

The currency risk exposure of domestic firms (Table 6.3.2) in Russia shows the same inverse relation with the exchange rate of the US Dollar as for the exporting firms, while we find a significantly positive relation with changes in the RUB/EUR rate. The Euro exposure, however, is substantially smaller, in absolute terms, than the exposure to the US Dollar, 0.029 compared to -0.342. For the CEEC-3 we do not find any significant exchange rate exposure for domestic firms at all.[84]

The results raise the question which channels – other than changes in firm's competitiveness – dominate for the CEEC-3. As mentioned in the introduction, mainly portfolio investments and foreign debt may cause a positive (but in the case of portfolio investments not necessarily causal) relation between the price of the domestic currency and the share price of exporting firms.[85] Unfortunately, both series are not available at high frequency but only on a yearly basis, so we cannot incorporate them into our model.

---

84 For both, exporting and domestic firms, the rolling regressions displayed in *Figures 6.1.1* and *6.1.2* show that the exposures are comparatively stable. For the significant coefficients in Tables 6.3.1 and 6.3.2 the 90% confidence interval remains almost permanently away from zero. Particularly in the case of Russia, the financial turmoil in 1998 (the Russian crisis) as well as in 2007/08 (the subprime crisis) is clearly visible. However, excluding these periods from the sample does not substantially change the results.

85 We also checked whether the difference can be due to an asymmetric exchange rate exposure (see Koutmos and Martin 2003) in combination with a long term exchange rate trend, since Poland and Hungary maintained a crawling peg for a substantial fraction of the sample period (Hungary until October 2001, Poland until April 2000), which led to a long-lasting depreciation of the domestic currency. However, although the exchange exposure is slightly higher, if the exchange rate depreciates (0.525 versus 0.458) the difference is small and not statistically significant.

Table 6.3.2: Portfolio results for domestic firms and exchange rate regimes

Results for the mean equation of a GJR (1,1) regression [(a)]									
	Russia		*CEEC-3*	*Czech Republic*		*Hungary*		*Poland*	
		Regime			*Regime*		*Regime*		*Regime*
c	0.000 (0.269)	0.000 (0.324)	0.000 (0.758)	0.000 (0.844)	0.000 (0.810)	**0.001***** **(0.000)**	**0.001***** **(0.000)**	0.000 (0.376)	0.000 (0.658)
Δe€	**0.029**** **(0.038)**	**0.043***** **(0.010)**	0.018 (0.136)	0.018 (0.136)	**0.024*** **(0.059)**	**0.199***** **(0.000)**	**-0.176***** **(0.000)**	**0.091***** **(0.000)**	**0.299***** **(0.000)**
Δe$	**-0.342***** **(0.000)**	**-0.375***** **(0.000)**	-0.009 (0.261)	-0.009 (0.261)	-0.009 (0.267)	**-0.022*** **(0.096)**	**0.027*** **(0.056)**	**0.043**** **(0.037)**	**0.071***** **(0.005)**
JAN	0.000 (0.728)	0.000 (0.728)	0.000 (0.254)	0.000 (0.254)	0.000 (0.257)	**0.001***** **(0.001)**	**0.001***** **(0.001)**	0.000 (0.672)	0.000 (0.998)
DEZ	**-0.001***** **(0.000)**	**0.000***** **(0.002)**	**0.001*** **(0.098)**	0.000 (0.822)	0.000 (0.823)	0.000 (0.593)	0.000 (0.597)	0.000 (0.805)	0.000 (0.988)
Euro 1999	**-0.001**** **(0.044)**	**-0.001*** **(0.083)**	0.000 (0.767)	**0.000**** **(0.026)**	**0.000**** **(0.023)**	**-0.001***** **(0.000)**	**-0.001***** **(0.000)**	0.000 (0.428)	0.000 (0.341)
EU 2004	**0.001***** **(0.000)**	**0.001***** **(0.000)**	0.000 (0.120)	0.000 (0.222)	0.000 (0.208)	**0.000***** **(0.047)**	**0.000**** **(0.048)**	**0.002***** **(0.001)**	**0.002***** **(0.000)**
fix $\Delta e_{€}$		0.022 (0.578)			-0.011 (0.772)		-0.029 (0.539)		**-0.285***** **(0.000)**
fix $\Delta e_{\$}$		**0.109***** **(0.000)**			-0.054 (0.233)		**-0.071*** **(0.068)**		-0.070 (0.390)
Adj. R^2	0.28	0.28	0.05	0.00	0.00	0.02	0.02	0.02	0.02
DW [(b)]	1.6	1.6	1.9	1.7	1.7	2.0	2.0	2.0	2.0

(a) The exchange rate is given in indirect quotation (foreign to domestic currency). Thus, a negative coefficient means that a depreciation (appreciation) of the domestic currency, or a decrease (increase) in the exchange rate, goes along with an increase (decrease) in share prices and vice versa. JAN, DEZ, Euro 1999, EU 2004 are the dummy variables as explained in Section 6.4. fix Δe€ and fix Δe$ are the interaction terms between exchange rate fluctuation and the exchange rate regime.

(b) Durbin Watson (DW) test

Stars refer to level of significance: * 10%, ** 5%, *** 1%

Figure 6.1.1: Rolling regressions for exposure of exporting firms

Russia

EUR

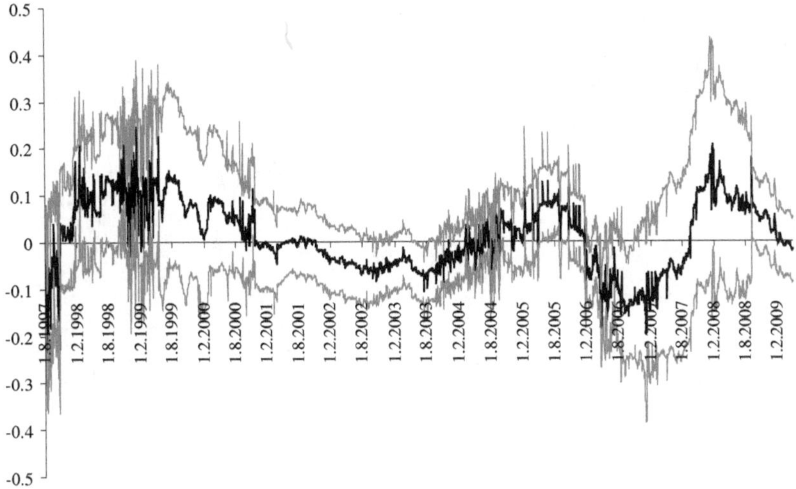

USD

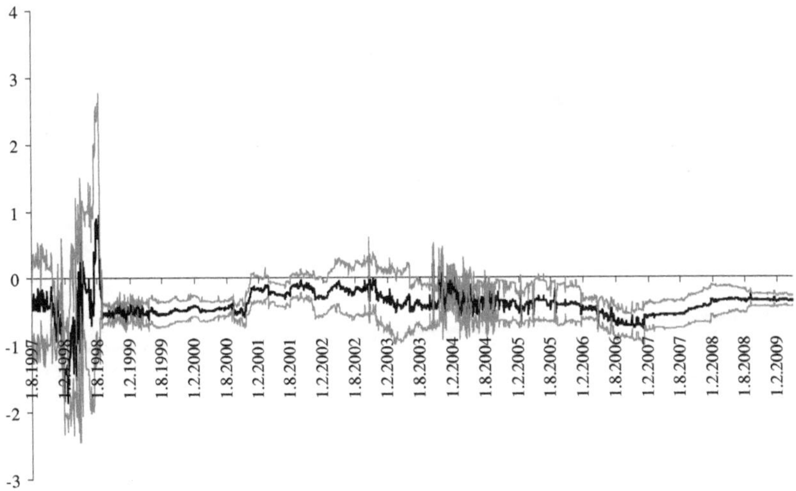

CEEC-3

EUR

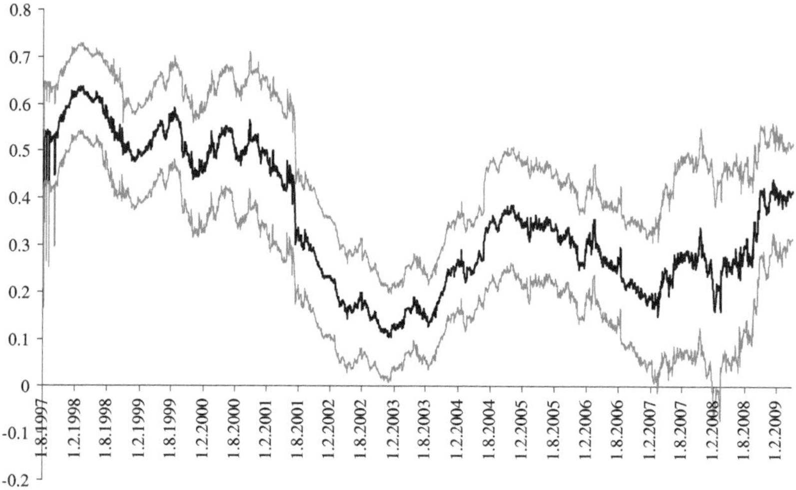

USD

Figure 6.1.2: Rolling regressions for exposure of domestic firms

Russia

EUR

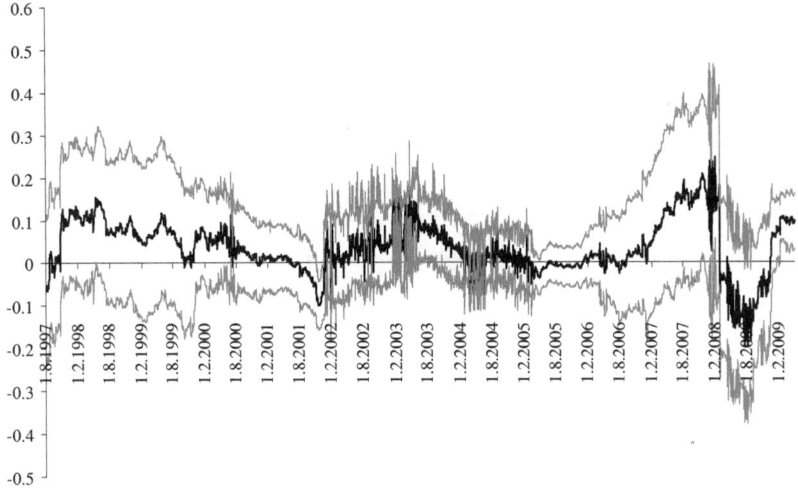

USD

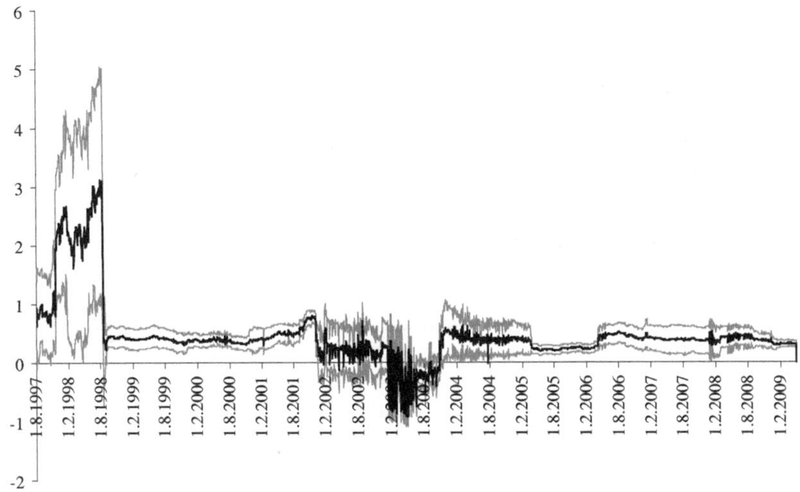

CEEC-3

EUR

USD

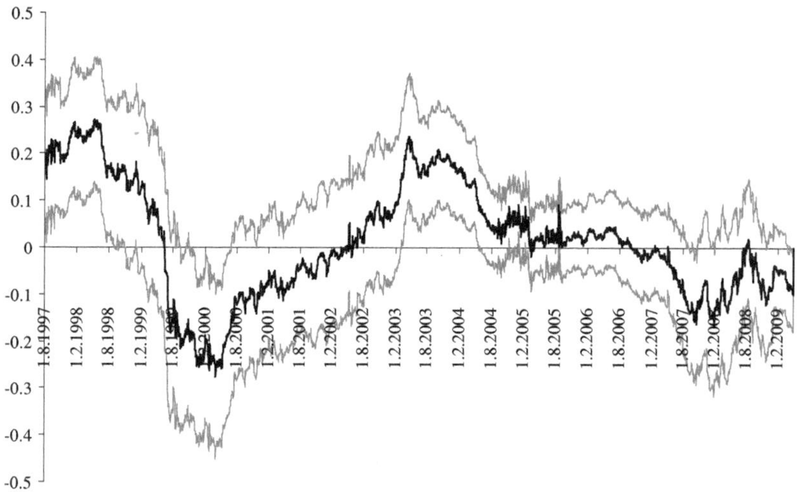

Note: The figures display the evolution of the coefficients $\gamma_{t,€}$ and $\gamma_{t,\$}$ respectively for a rolling regression over a window of 500 observations.

Figure 6.2: Inflow of portfolio investments in equity in % of market capitalization

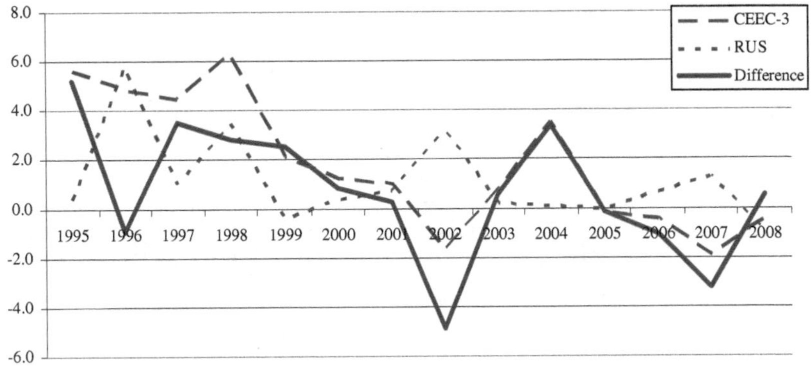

Source: EBRD, World Bank

Figure 6.2 shows the evolution of inflows of portfolio investments for Russia and the CEEC-3 calculated as per cent of the stock market capitalization. It serves as a measure of the dependence of the stock market on foreign investors. The difference is comparatively small, although the CEEC-3 show a slightly higher share of foreign investors, particularly in the first half of the sample period. It seems to be unlikely that this difference is responsible for the huge difference in foreign exchange risk exposures between the CEEC-3 and Russia.

In contrast, the difference in the amount of foreign debt, as displayed in *Figure 6.3*, is much larger.[86] While all countries but the Czech Republic show a substantial increase in private external debt (most pronounced for Hungary, where the foreign debt quadrupled during the sample period), the levels are different: in Russia it increased smoothly to a moderate level of slightly more than 20% of GDP in 2009. In the CEEC-3, the share of foreign debt is substantially higher (peaking at 80% of GDP for Hungary) and sharply increasing in Hungary and Poland. Therefore, due to their high exposure to foreign debt, the CEEC-3 seem to be much more vulnerable to currency risk than Russia.

86 Unfortunately, there is no data available on the share of foreign debt in total corporate debt. We therefore rely on external debt of the private sector, which includes besides corporate debt also debt of private households.

Figure 6.3: Private sector external debt in % of GDP [(a)(b)]

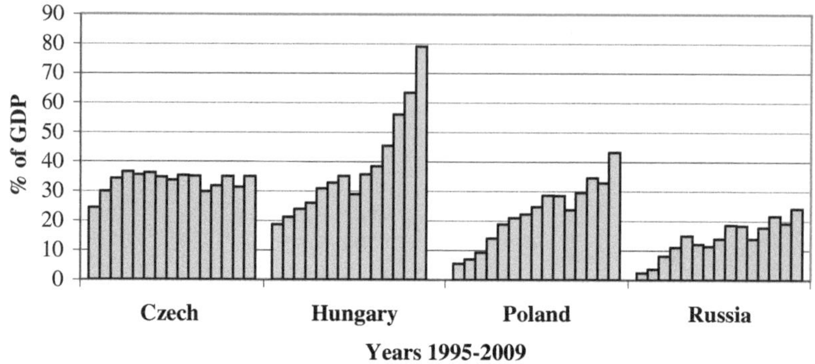

(a) Private Sector External Debt is calculated as the difference of the Gross External Debt (as it is defined by international organizations IMF, OECD, World Bank) and Public Sector External Debt (including General Government, Monetary Authorities, and other non-financial or financial corporations which are subject to control by government and monetary authorities). Thus, Private Sector External Debt excludes equity and financial derivative instruments from external debt.

(b) For Hungary, the data for 2009 was not yet available.

Source: National Central Banks, EUROSTAT, IMF

The regressions in Tables 6.3.1 and 6.3.2 additionally include an interaction term between the exposure and the dummy variable on the exchange rate regime, according to equation (3). The results, however, are mixed and not clear. Although we find a significant relation between the exchange rate regime and exchange rate exposure of exporting firms for Poland (USD and EUR), the Czech Republic and Hungary (both only USD) and of domestic firms for Poland (EUR), Hungary (USD) and Russia (USD), the signs of the coefficients differ and do not show a clear pattern. We therefore conclude that, at best, the exchange rate regime plays a minor role for the exchange rate exposure of firms.

Since the empirical literature suggests that estimations on the firm level provide clearer results than on the aggregate level (Khoo, 1994, Choi and Prasad, 1995, Muller and Verschoor, 2006b), we additionally estimate equation (1) on the firm level. The results are given in *Table 6.4.1* for exporting and *6.4.2* for domestic firms. They confirm and strengthen our insights from the aggregate level (Tables 6.3.1 and 6.3.2).

Table 6.4.1: Exchange rate exposure for single stocks of exporting firms [(a)]

	Coefficients of the GJR (1,1) regression (Tab.6.3)					
	Mean	Median	Min	Max	positive (significant)	negative (significant)
Russia						
EUR	0.043	-0.017	-0.217	1.681	13 (2)	17 (4)
USD	-0.301	-0.350	-0.747	1.658	2 (1)	28 (25)
CEEC-3						
EUR	0.265	0.241	-0.073	1.107	19 (18)	2 (0)
USD	0.020	0.015	-0.173	0.222	12 (8)	9 (4)

Table 6.4.2: Exchange rate exposure for single stocks of domestic firms [(a)]

	Coefficients of the GJR (1,1) regression (Tab.6.3)					
	Mean	Median	Min	Max	positive (significant)	negative (significant)
Russia						
EUR	0.013	0.011	-1.141	0.615	30 (16)	28 (14)
USD	-0.303	-0.327	-0.736	0.276	6 (4)	52 (43)
CEEC-3						
EUR	0.273	0.303	-0.050	0.818	31 (24)	2 (0)
USD	0.023	0.000	-0.142	0.337	16 (7)	17 (6)

(a) The exchange rate is given in indirect quotation (foreign to domestic currency). Thus, a negative coefficient means that a depreciation (appreciation) of the domestic currency, or a decrease (increase) in the exchange rate, goes along with an increase (decrease) in share prices and vice versa.

For Russia 28 out of 30 exporting firms show a negative coefficient for the USD/RUB rate, 25 of them being significant. From the only two firms with a positive exposure, one is significant.[87] The exposure of Russian exporting firms

87 This single Russian exporting firm with a significantly positive exposure is Mechel OAO, Russia's largest exporter of coking coal concentrate, having an exchange rate exposure of 1.681 to Euro and of 1.658 to the US Dollar. We resisted the temptation to re-

to changes in the Euro rate is almost equally distributed (17 negative, 13 positive) and insignificant in most cases. While the distribution for Russian domestic firms looks similar, the share of significant exposures to the Euro rate is about 50%, still without any clear direction.

Again, the CEEC-3 present a very different picture: 19 (18 of them being significant) out of 21 exporting firms show a positive relation with the Euro exchange rate. The exposure to the US Dollar exchange rate is less pronounced, but a slight majority of firms also shows positive coefficients. In contrast to the aggregate level, the domestic firms also show a more pronounced positive exposure to the Euro exchange rate (31 out of 33, 24 being significant).

6.6 Conclusion

This paper extends the scarce literature on foreign exchange exposure in Eastern European transition markets by examining the relationship between their exporting firms' stock returns and fluctuations in both, the US Dollar and Euro exchange rates. In particular, we focus on the four transition economies Czech Republic, Hungary, Poland (CEEC-3) and Russia in the period from September 1995 to April 2009.

In both, Russia and the CEEC-3, we find clear and economically significant, but different patterns of exposure to the two reference currencies. (1) In Russia, 80% of exporting firms exhibit a strong and negative exposure to the US Dollar rate, meaning that a depreciation of domestic currency against the US Dollar goes along with an increase of exporting firms' share prices. This result indicates a dominant effect arising through the competitiveness channel. Thereby, the exposure to the Euro is mixed and significant only for 20% of Russian firms. (2) By contrast, in the CEEC-3, 86% of exporting firms display a strong and positive exposure to the Euro rate and only a slight one to the US Dollar, which can rather be explained by the foreign debt channel. (3) Furthermore, we find that the exchange rate regime does not seem to be substantially relevant for share prices.

Our results provide one possible explanation for why many empirical studies fail to find a clear exchange rate exposure (see e.g. the survey by Muller and Verschoor, 2006a). Since most of these studies include firms from a variety of countries, the poor results may be partly due to the disappearance of separated country-specific effects in cross-country samples. In our sample, this would

---

categorize this company and kept in the set of exporting firms, leaving our results more conservative.

mean that the revealed opposite signs of exposures in Russia and the CEEC-3 are likely to cancel out in a joint sample.

Moreover, finding exporting firms not always feature a negative exposure to foreign exchange movements, investors should be aware that investments in exporting firms are not always a good hedge against foreign exchange risk. Our results show that the direction of the exposure to the US Dollar and Euro varies in different economies. Being a US investor in Russia, the foreign exchange risk (of an investment in Ruble) can be partly hedged by buying stocks of Russian exporting firms. The latter would at least compensate for a depreciation of the Ruble by increasing share prices. However, this hedging effect would not exist for a Euro-zone investor in the CEEC-3. By contrast, as in the CEEC-3 the exposure of exporting firms to the Euro is positive, a depreciation of the CEEC-3 currencies against the Euro goes along with decreasing share prices of exporting firms. Therefore, this effect would even more reduce the profits from holding CEEC-3 exporting firms. For the US Dollar, the exposure is much weaker but not clear in direction. Thus, investors should distinguish these country- and currency-specific effects, when aiming to hedge their foreign investments against foreign exchange risk.

Finally, one potential reason for the found opposite exposures in our two sub-samples might be the varying dominance of the exposure transmission channels in Russia and the CEEC-3. We may assume all the three channels – influencing share prices through the competitiveness, the foreign debt or portfolio investments – to have some impact. However, in particular the dominance of the competitiveness channel in Russia suggests the structure of exports to be of particular relevance here. Russia mostly exports homogeneous goods like oil and gas (according to the Statistical Office of the Russian Federation, mineral products account for almost two third of Russian exports), which price is in USD as well as largely determined by the world market and not by the firm itself. This makes Russian exporting firms more vulnerable to changes in the exchange rate, which directly affect their profits. Exporting mostly not fully homogeneous industrial products (according to the EBRD, over 50% of total CEEC-3 exports are sold to the EU, thus generating revenues in EUR), the firms in the CEEC-3 might be able to adjust their prices to their domestic currency price fluctuations. Thus, assuming that exporting homogeneous goods (like oil and gas) provides fewer opportunities to compensate for lost profits (due to currency risk) by price adjustments, the exposure to exchange rate fluctuations rises and gets more negative. This view provides an alternative explanation for Russian exporters' high exposure to the USD/RUB rate fluctuations and, thus, for a strong competitiveness channel in

Russia. However, although exchange rate exposure has "many facets" (Bartram et al., 2010), we retrieve remarkably stable results per country group.

Summing up, our results allow for relevant conclusions and implications from both the practical and the academic perspective. Investors should take into account that there are differing country-specific exposures to exchange rates of the same foreign currency. It is also due to the latter why researchers should not merge (economically) differing economies in just one sample, because otherwise country-specific exposures, which result from a country's individual economic and export structure, might cancel each other out. This would hinder the detection of a clear exchange rate exposure.

Appendix: Information on exporting companies (taken from annual reports 2008)

(a) Export share is given as % of total sales in 2008. If this data was not available, the information in "About the company" taken from the respective company's homepage discloses why a company has been defined as an exporting firm (see italic marking).

Name Code	Sector	About the company	Export share [a]	Export to:
Czech Republic				
PEGAS NON-WOVENS CZ:PEN(P)	Nonwoven textiles	Production of synthetic nonwoven textiles from polypropylene or poly-ethylene filaments.	80%	Western Europe, Central and Eastern Europe, Russia, other
PHILIP MORRIS ČR CZ:TAB(P)	Tobacco products	Leading international tobacco company. 15.6% share of the international cigarette market outside of the USA in 2008.	59%	160 countries
SPOLEK CHEM.HUT.V. CZ:SPC(P)	Chemicals	The Company exports and imports a significant portion of products (che-mical substances and chemical pre-parations) and raw materials and is therefore significantly exposed to foreign exchange risk arising from various currency exposures primarily with respect to the Euro.	85%	UK, USA, Western Europe, (Germany, Netherlands, France, Italy, Sweden, Great Britain, Austria, Switzerland, Spain, Belgium), Poland, Slovakia, Turkey
UNIPETROL CZ:UNP(P)	Crude oil processing, production of petro-chemical products	Production and sale of refinery products, chemical and petrochemical products, polymers, fertilizers, and specialty chemicals, retail distribution of motor fuels. Business based on exports and imports was significantly affected by the trends in currency exchange rates. Since 2005, part of Central Europe's largest refining and petrochemical group, PKN Orlen.	44% (2006), 29% (2007)	Central and Eastern Europe (Poland, Slovakia, Germany, Austria, Czech Republic)
Hungary				
EGIS HN:EGI(P)	Pharmaceuticals	Manufacture and distribution of generic drugs and their active ingredients. In December 1995, France Servier SAS acquired 50.9 percent of the company shares.	approx. 60%	CIS states, other Eastern Europ. countries, Western Europe, USA

LINAMAR HN:LMH(P)	Engineering and machinery	One of the largest Hungarian agricultural machinery manufacturers. Also manufactures and distributes harvesting equipment, precision-made parts, primarily to the automotive industry. A subsidiary of the Canadian Linamar Corp.	88%	European Union and non-EU, North America, other
MOL HN:MMG(P)	Oil and natural gas industry	Major Central European company in the integrated oil and gas industry and largest enterprise in Hungary (turnover), founded in 1991. Dominant shareholder in Slovnaft, the leading Slovakian oil industry company (proportion of shares 98.4% in 2004), also of the Croatian company INA (25% in 2003). Market leader in its main activities both in Hungary and Slovakia. A substantial part of MOL s natural gas division has been sold, except for its natural gas transportation division. Strategic partnership with Gazprom since 2006.	57%	Operation in 10 Eastern European and Asian countries
PANNERGY HN:PAN(P)	Renewable energy, packaging industry	Investment and operating activities in the renewable energy resources sector, primarily geothermal energy. Plastic processing mainly for packaging industry, manufacturing of composite insulator.	58%	European Union (also Ukraine, Serbia)
RICHTER HN:RIC(P)	Pharmaceuticals	Manufacturing and distribution of active ingredients and generic pharmaceuticals. Since 1997, the largest domestic drug manufacturer.	81%	European Union, USA, CIS, Japan, other
TVK HN:TVK(P)	Chemicals	Production of ethylene and propylene from purchased naphtha and gasoil. A member of the MOL Group (94.86% of the company shares are owned indirectly by MOL). Legal predecessor was founded in 1953. One of the biggest integrated olefin and polyolefin producers in Europe.	48%	Germany, Italy, Poland, Austria, UK, France
Poland				
AMICA PO:AMI	Electro-engineering	Manufacture of cookers, launch, heating equipment. One of the most modern washing machine factories in Europe. Danish manufacturing and trading company.	over 50%	Eastern and Scandinavian market
BIOTON PO:BIO(P)	Pharma-ceuticals, chemcals	Pharmaceutical enterprise that produces modern medicine: recombined human insulin and antibiotics.	41% (2007); 32% (2008)	Russia, Asia, Chinese market (also Euro-zone and CEEC)

BUDIMEX PO:BUX	Construction	Exports of construction services primarily to the developing markets of Asia and Africa and the COMECON. A leading construction company in Poland. A joint stock company. The Ferrovial Group, a strategic investor based in Spain, has been holding more than 50% of share capital and votes in the General Meeting since 2000. The fusion of the investing capacity, know-how, market position, and international experience of Ferrovial with contacts in Poland and CEE markets provided new opportunities and helped expansion into other business areas.	80%	Germany (also Russia, Belarus and Ukraine)
CERSANIT PO:CER(P)	Building materials	Industry Building materials: national leader in the area of complex bathroom outfitting, strongly expanding the range of its export activity. Production and sales of sanitary ware products, ceramic tiles, shower cabins, acrylic bathtubs, acrylic wading paddles, bathroom furniture as well as other bathroom fixtures.	40%	
DEBICA PO:DEB	Automobiles	Automobiles: the leading Polish maker of passenger and commercial tires, all-steel truck tires, off-road tires, for agricultural machinery and other products from the tire industry.	76%	Germany, Slovenia, France, Russia, Italy, England, Romania, Spain and United Arab Emirates, also UK, USA, Brazil (60 countries)
KABLE HOLDING PO:SLA	Electro-engineering	With manufacturing facilities in Denmark, Germany, Norway, the Czech Republic, Poland and China and sales offices all over the world, nkt cables is a market oriented, highly technological cables manufacturer with global ambitions. Provider of numerous consulting and engineering services. Owned by Danish NKT Holding A/S.	80%	Eastern Europe, Germany, Denmark, Asia, other
KETY PO:KET	Metals	Aluminium industry. *Exports 33% of its products.*		Europe
KGHM PO:KGH(P)	Metals	One of the largest Polish exporters, the 7th-largest copper producer and the 3rd-largest silver producer in the world. The electrolytic copper produced by KGHM is registered by the London Metal Exchange as "Grade A". It produces also gold, lead, sulphuric acid and rock salt.	70%	Copper: China, France, Germany and the Czech Rep.. Silver: GB, Belgium, Germany, USA.

MONDIE SWIECIE PO:MPP	Wood & paper	High quality containerboard and sack paper producer. One of five major packaging paper producers for European paper sack and corrugated board industries.	74%	Benelux, Great Britain, France, Sweden, other
POLIMEXMS PO:PXM(P)	Construction and installation services	*One of the biggest* manufacturers and *exporters of steel products* and platform gratings *in Poland*, leader in the Polish engineering and construction sector. General contractor in the following sectors: power engineering, chemical, petrochemical and environmental protection.		European market
STOMIL PO:SAN	Chemicals, automobiles	*An enterprise active on European markets.* Producer of rubber, rubber to metal goods, rubber to plastic and TPE goods used in car body sealing systems, car suspension and exhaust suspension systems, electrical, power transmission, fuel and cooling systems.		Germany, Belgium, Belarus, Russia, other.
Russia				
ACRON RS:ACR	Chemical production	A leading Russian and global mineral fertiliser producer (multi-nutrient fertilisers such as NPK and bulk blends, as well as straight nitrogen-based products such as urea, ammonium nitrate and UAN).	70%	China, Latin America, Asia, former USSR (over 50 countries)
CHELYABIN SK MTL.PLT. RS:CMF	Metals and mining	Part of Mechel's steel business. Mechel is one of the leading Russian mining and metals companies (mining, steel, ferroalloys and power), the largest Russian producer of special steel, the second largest Russian producer of long steel products as well.	46%	
GAZPROM RS:GAZ	Oil & gas, natural gas sales	The world's largest natural gas company controlling a quarter of the world's total gas reserves. Key supplier of gas to Europe and the CIS, engaged in several transcontinental gas infrastructure projects. Russia's largest company by turnover and market capitalisation. 50, 01% state-owned. Supplies approx. one third of Western Europe's total gas imports (about 60% of revenues).	60%	Germany, Italy, Turkey, France, CIS (32 countries)
GAZPROM NEFT RS:SIB	Oil & gas, oil sales	One of the largest oil and gas producing companies in Russia. The main areas of Gazprom Neft's business activity include oil and natural gas production, oil and gas field facility services, oil refining and		Germany, Italy, Turkey, France, CIS (32 countries)

		marketing of petroleum products. The proven reserves of the company exceed 6,9 billion barrels, which ranks the company *amongst the world's twenty largest oil companies.*	
IRKUT RS:SPC	Machinery	Aircraft-manufacturing corporation, capable of accomplishing research-and-development, manufacturing, after-sales support, and upgrades of top-of-the-line aircraft ranging from civil and military aircraft to avionics and ground equipment. Accounts for over 15% of Russia's defense export. *The best Russian Exporter 2008.*	37 countries
MAGNITO-GORSK IOSTL. WORKS RS:MAG	Metals and mining	The Magnitogorsk Iron and Steel Works Open Joint Stock Company (MMK) is one of the largest enterprises of the Russian steel sector accounting for about 20% of all steel products sold on the Russian market. *50% of products are sold in the export.*	South East Asia, Middle East, Africa, Belarus, Ukraine, Kazakhstan, other CIS states (60 countries)
MECHEL OAO RS:MSG	Metals and mining	One of the leading Russian mining and metals companies (mining, steel, ferroalloys and electric and heat power). *Russia's largest exporter of coking coal concentrate.* Second largest producer of coking coal in Russia, controls 23% of the coking coal washing capacity in Russia. Subsidiaries in Kazakhstan, USA, Romania, Bulgaria and Lithuania. *Products are sold in Russia as well as on international markets.* Mechel is the only coal mining and metals company in the region of Eastern and Central Europe and Russia having its shares placed on the NYSE.	International markets (Kazakhstan, USA, Romania, Bulgaria and Lithuania)
MMC NORILSK NICKEL RS:GMK	Metals and mining	Mining and Metallurgical Company Norilsk Nickel (hereinafter - MMC Norilsk Nickel or the Company) and its subsidiaries (hereinafter - the Group) is the *world's leading producer of nickel and palladium,* and one of the *largest global producers of platinum and copper.* The Group also produces a variety of by-products, such as cobalt, rhodium, silver, gold, iridium, ruthenium, selenium, tellurium and sulfur. The world's leading producer of nickel, copper, and palladium, among other strategic metals. One of the most international of the Russian companies.	Australia, Botswana, Finland, the United States of America and South Africa.

NIZHNE-KAMSK-NEFTEKHIM RS:NKN	Oil, chemical production	High-tech petrochemical company producing rubber, plastics, monomers as feedstock to produce rubber and plastics, other petrochemical products.	53%	Europe, South-East Asia, America (50 countries)
NOVATEK RS:NTV	Oil & gas	*Russia's largest independent gas producer* and second-largest natural gas producer. Russia's leading independent gas producer. 25% owned by Gazprom. Responsible for a major part of Russia's gas production growth in recent years. Some 5% of Russia's gas production and a similar share of gas reserves. Securing access to Gazprom-controlled gas transportation infrastructure and *to export pipelines* in particular.	72% (2007), 64% (2006)	
NOVOLIPETSK STEEL RS:NFM	Metals and mining	One of the world's largest steel producers. An integrated steel-making company, we produce pig iron, slabs, hot-rolled, cold-rolled, galvanised, pre-painted, transformer and dynamo steel. It has won the 2007 Best Russian Exporter contest in the category of Ferrous Metals Best Exporter in the Industry.	90% (2007)	Europe, America, Asia, Africa and the Middle East (70 countries)
NVYSK.COML.SEA PORT RS:NVR	Transport	Novorossiysk Commercial Sea Port ("NCSP") is a multi-purpose Russian stevedoring and port services company and Russia's largest commercial sea port operator, according to Global Insight/ISL. NCSP is a key gateway for shipment of a wide range of Russian import and export cargoes, handling approximately 20% of Russia's exports and imports shipped via sea port during 2006, according to the Association of Russian Sea Ports. NCSP operates primarily at the Port of Novorossiysk (the "Port"), a multi-purpose, year-round, deep-water port located on the Russian shore of the Black Sea.	48%	
OC ROSNEFT RS:RSF	Oil & gas	Leader of Russia's petroleum industry, ranks among the world's top publicly traded oil and gas companies. Russia's largest oil producer (also by market capitalisation), 100% state-owned. Acquired the core of the former oil company Yukos' assets in 2005. 25% of Russia's oil output, 2-3% of the world's reserves.	62%	Europe, CIS

OGK-2 RS:WHL	Electric utilities	The Open Joint-Stock Second Generation Company of the wholesale electricity market, abbreviated title: JSC "OGK-2". *Exporting electricity to neighbouring CIS countries and along a transit route to Western-European countries.*		Western-European and neighbouring CIS countries (Georgia and Azerbaijan)
OMZ URALMASH IZHORA GP. RS:UMA	Production sector	OMZ (Uralmash-Izhora Group) is the largest heavy industry company in Russia. It specializes in engineering, production, sales and maintenance of equipment and machines for the nuclear power, oil and gas, and mining industries, and also in the production of special steels and equipment for other industries.	over 50%	Asia, Europe, CIS
LUKOIL (JSC) RS:LKO	Oil & gas	The 6th largest non-state publicly traded oil company worldwide by production of hydrocarbons. Russia's 2nd largest oil producer. 2-3% of global oil reserves, 2.3% of global oil production, 20% of Russia's oil output. The company with second largest trading volumes among foreign companies traded on the London Stock Exchange (IOB) in 2008. The only private Russian oil company whose share capital is dominated by minority stakeholders. The most international among the Russian companies. Russia's largest oil exporter.	aprox. 64%	CIS, the Baltic States, Finland, South-Eastern Europe, other
POLYMETAL RS:POL	Metals and mining	Polymetal is a leading precious metals mining company. Polymetal is one of the top ten silver producers in the world and the largest in Russia.	72%	
POLYUS GOLD RS:PYG	Metals and mining	Polyus Gold (Open Joint Stock Company, OJSC) is a leading gold producer. The sales structure changed significantly. 2006: export accounted for almost 30% of sales. 2007: gold was largely sold in the domestic market to Russian banks (87% of sales). The increase of sales in the domestic market is explained by more favorable contracts terms concluded with Russian banks.	30% (2006)	Credit Suisse (Zurich, Switzerland)
RASPADSKA -YA RS:RAS	Metals and mining	Raspadskaya is a compact integrated coal mining and enrichment complex. One of the leading suppliers to the largest Russian smelters, including Novolipetsk Steel, Magnitogorsk Iron & Steel Works and Nizhniy Tagil Iron & Steel Works.	approx. 32 %	Eastern Europe (Ukraine, Romania, Hungry, Bulgaria), South-Asia (India, Japan and South Korea)

SEVERSTAL RS:CHM	Metals and mining	The 12th largest steel producer in the world, a steel leader in Russia and the CIS. Integrated steel and mining business model worldwide, mining segment is one of Russia's three largest producers of iron ore concentrate (with a market share of 9.1%), pellets (30%) and coking coal (14,7%). The company's revenues grew by nearly 50% in 2008, the strongest performance among the key Russian metal companies. Through a series of acquisitions in 2008, Severstal entered the gold mining industry and aims to become one of the leading producers in Russia.	53%	Europe and Asia; USA, Central and South America, Africa, Middle East, Europe, Central and South East Asia
SLAVNEFT MEGIONNEF TEGAZ RS:MFG	Oil & gas	The Group's principal activities are the extraction, production of oil and gas.	47%	
SURGUT-NEFTEGAS RS:SNG; SURGUT-NEFTEGAZ PREF. RS:SNP	Oil & gas	One of the largest oil companies in Russia. Prospecting, gas- and oil-field construction and development, oil and gas production and marketing, oil and petrochemical products producing and marketing come within the scope of the company's activities. *Export of crude oil and petroleum products: 55% and 61% in 2006.*		CIS and Western Europe
TMK OAO RS:TUE	Production sector	One of the world's largest oil and gas pipe producers and the market leader of the Russian pipe industry. Shipments of longitudinal welded large-diameter pipes for the Russian part of the Eastern Siberia–Pacific Ocean (ESPO) oil pipeline spur to China. TMK is *Russia's largest exporter of pipe products*, accounting for about 52% of all Russian steel pipe exports.		Europe, Middle East, North Africa, South and South-East Asia, CIS (over 60 countries)
TRANSNEFT PREF. RS:TRP	Oil & gas, oil transporting	Transneft is Russia's primary crude oil export channel. Its network is fully interconnected with the European pipeline system.	approx. 60%	Ukraine, Belarus, Baltic countries, North America and Europe
UDMURTNEF T PREF. RS:UDP	Oil & gas	Largest oil-producing enterprise in the Udmurt Republic. Holds 60 hydrocarbon exploration and production licenses. Rosneft indirectly holds 49.51% in Udmurtneft.	63,6%	China, Europe

UFA ENGINE PLANT RS:UFM	Production sector	Production and service of the turbo-jet aviamotors.	over 70%	49 countries (e.i. Vietnam)
URALKALIY RS:URK	Chemical production	One of the world's leading producers of potash fertiliser and one of Russia's largest chemical companies. Primarily an export business. Sales to customers in Russia account for around 10% of production. Leading market position in developing markets.	89%	China, Brazil, South-East Asia and India, also Europe, Africa, the Middle East and USA
VSMPO RS:VS	Metals and mining	The world's largest manufacturer of titanium - ingots and all kinds of semi finished items from titanium alloys. *More than three quarters of company output is exported* mainly to large world aircraft manufacturer such as Boeing, EADS/Airbus, General Electric.		more than 350 firms in 50 countries
WIMM-BILL-DANN FOODS RS:WBD	Food industry	Market leader in dairy products and children's food in Russia and one of the *leading players in the market* for non-alcoholic drinks in Russia *and the CIS.* A three-time recipient of "*The Best Industry Sector Exporter*" award of the Russian Ministry of Economic Development. Export of "Essentuki" mineral water. Around 280 million people in Russia, Ukraine, Belarus and the countries of Central Asia buy Wimm-Bill-Dann's products.		USA, Canada, France, China, Mongolia, Israel, Latvia, Estonia, Lithuania, Moldova, Ukraine, Belarus, Kazakhstan, Georgia, Armenia

Annex: Questionnaire

International Survey in Professional Asset Management

By answering this questionnaire you are supporting an academic research project, which focuses on the personal viewpoints, perceptions and investment behavior of professional asset managers. Please fill in this questionnaire and send it to (address and email) by (deadline).

We would kindly ask you to answer the following questions completely and truthfully. This data will be kept in strictest confidence and anonymity. Besides, we will provide the results of our analysis to you on request.

Personal Data

Gender: ☐ Male ☐ Female

Marital status: ☐ Single ☐ Married ☐ Other

How old are you?
☐ < 31 ☐ 31 - 35 ☐ 36 - 40 ☐ 41 - 45 ☐ 46 - 50 ☐ > 50

Professional experience in asset management (in years):
☐ < 4 ☐ 4 - 6 ☐ 7 - 9 ☐ 10 - 12 ☐ 13 - 15 ☐ > 15

Average working hours per week:
☐ < 41 ☐ 41 - 45 ☐ 46 - 50 ☐ 51 - 55 ☐ 56 - 60 ☐ > 60

Average period of data procurement and research: __ Hours per week

Educational level: ☐ Non-academic education ☐ Academic education

Current position within your company:
☐ Junior Asset Manager ☐ Senior Asset Manager
☐ Head of AM team ☐ CIO / CEO

Average bonus you receive in addition to your fixed salary: ___ %

Type of managed fund: ☐ Mutual fund ☐ Restricted / special / pension fund

Major investment segment: ☐ Equities ☐ Bonds ☐ Money market

Your company's total volume of assets under management (in billion of $):
☐ < 5 ☐ 5 - 10 ☐ 10- 20 ☐ 20 - 50 ☐ 50 - 100 ☐ > 100

Your personal responsibility for assets under management (in million of $):
☐ < 50 ☐ 50 - 250 ☐ 250-1,000 ☐ 1,000 – 2,500 ☐ 2,500 - 10,000 ☐ > 10,000

Performance Incentives

Do you get a share participation option plan / stock option programme? ☐ Yes ☐ No

If you receive a performance-based remuneration, which criteria determine the size of that bonus?

	highest relevance					no relevance
Absolute fund performance	☐	☐	☐	☐	☐	☐
Relative fund performance	☐	☐	☐	☐	☐	☐
Business development of the investment company	☐	☐	☐	☐	☐	☐
Subjective assessment by superiors and colleagues	☐	☐	☐	☐	☐	☐

Please describe your investment performance and assess your achievement in asset management:

	much better						much worse
How was your risk-adjusted performance last year – compared to other asset managers' performance in the same investment segment?	☐	☐	☐	☐	☐	☐	☐
How do you assess your achievement in asset management – compared to other asset managers' achievement in the same investment segment?	☐	☐	☐	☐	☐	☐	☐

Your opinion on the general behavior of asset managers

Please assess the investment behavior of professional asset managers:

	complete approval					complete contradiction
People are not machines; thus security prices are clearly more determined by psychological influences than by fundamentals.	☐	☐	☐	☐	☐	☐
Herding is observable amongst professional asset managers.	☐	☐	☐	☐	☐	☐
Asset Managers often disregard some information, if it does not complement their opinion.	☐	☐	☐	☐	☐	☐
Following the herd benefits the asset manager's career.	☐	☐	☐	☐	☐	☐

Your personal investment behavior and information processing

Please describe your investment behavior by responding to the following statements:	complete approval					complete contradiction
I prefer to take profits instead of cutting losses, when I am confronted with unexpected liquidity demands.	☐	☐	☐	☐	☐	☐
As a domestic asset manager I benefit from better information on domestic securities compared to market players overseas.	☐	☐	☐	☐	☐	☐
I often trade too much, as my clients demand short-term performance.	☐	☐	☐	☐	☐	☐
Most of the published business news does not surprise me at all.	☐	☐	☐	☐	☐	☐
In case of loss positions in my portfolio I generally wait for a price rebound instead of selling those securities.	☐	☐	☐	☐	☐	☐
I generally follow the trend.	☐	☐	☐	☐	☐	☐

What is your personal forecasting horizon when making investment decisions?

☐ Days ☐ Weeks ☐ 2-6 Months ☐ 6-12 Months ☐ Years

Please assess the following sources of information used in making investment decision:	highest relevance					no relevance
Fundamental facts about the company / market	☐	☐	☐	☐	☐	☐
Chart analysis / technical indicators	☐	☐	☐	☐	☐	☐
Discussions / exchange of views with colleagues	☐	☐	☐	☐	☐	☐
Investments decisions of other market players	☐	☐	☐	☐	☐	☐
Statements of opinion leaders within the industry (e.g. Warren Buffett)	☐	☐	☐	☐	☐	☐
Statements of economic opinion leaders (e.g. Alan Greenspan, Wim Duisenberg)	☐	☐	☐	☐	☐	☐

Please describe your management style:

	high tracking error					Indexing
How actively (i.e. high tracking error) can you manage your portfolio at most?	☐	☐	☐	☐	☐	☐
How actively (i.e. high tracking error) do you manage your portfolio in fact?	☐	☐	☐	☐	☐	☐

Please classify your personal risk-taking:

	very risk averse					little risk averse
In respect of professional investment decisions, I mostly act…	☐	☐	☐	☐	☐	☐

Which strategies are your investment decisions normally based upon?

Please assign **100 % altogether**. If a category does not apply at all, please assign 0 % to it.

___ % Momentum Strategy ___ % Buy-and-Hold Strategy ___ % Others

___ % Contrarian Strategy ___ % Dividend-oriented Strategy

How much importance do you attach to the following categories of information?

Please assign **100 % altogether**. If a category does not apply at all, please assign 0 % to it.

___ % **Fundamentals** (economic and political hard facts)
___ % **Technical analysis** (charts and quantitative indicators)
___ % **(Order) Flows** (observed transactions)

What is your personal forecasting horizon when using this information?

Fundamentals:	☐ Intraday	☐ Days	☐ Weeks	☐ 2-6 Months	☐ 6-12 Months	☐ Years
Technical Analysis:	☐ Intraday	☐ Days	☐ Weeks	☐ 2-6 Months	☐ 6-12 Months	☐ Years
(Order) Flows:	☐ Intraday	☐ Days	☐ Weeks	☐ 2-6 Months	☐ 6-12 Months	☐ Years

Apart from any fund's restriction – Imagine your portfolio's performance differs from its benchmark near the end of the period.

If my portfolio has outperformed its benchmark so far, I would...

- ☐ increase the relative risk level to become a top performer
- ☐ decrease the relative risk level to lock in the performance
- ☐ not change my strategy

If my portfolio has underperformed its benchmark so far, I would...

- ☐ increase the relative risk level to reach the benchmark
- ☐ decrease the relative risk level to avoid further deficits
- ☐ not change my strategy

Imagine someone offers you a bet and the odds are fifty-fifty. You will have to pay 1000 $ from your personal account, if you lose. What would be the minimum amount you would expect to win to lure you into accepting the bet?

At least _____ $.

Please estimate the development of the *(home stock index),* **the Dow Jones and the EuroSTOXX 50 within the next month.** Please forecast the performance of the respective index with a probability of 90 %:

Date: __.__.200_ (mm/dd)	**Home stock index**	**Dow Jones**	**EuroSTOXX 50**
Today's level:			
Expected minimum level:			
Expected maximum level:			

Thank you very much for your participation!

Country-specific adaptations:

1) Question posed only in USA and Germany:

"Do you get a share participation option plan / stock option programme?"

Due to missing evidence, this question on performance incentives was excluded from the Russian, Ukrainian, and Thai questionnaires after pre-survey interviews with fund managers.

2) Additional question for surveys in Germany and Thailand – presented in the version for Germany:

What are your long-term expectations for the next 10 years?

Even if it is difficult to forecast long-term developments, we would like to ask you to estimate the respective development within the next 10 years (in per cent).

		Germany	Europe	USA	Asia
Stock market	average stock yield per year (in percent):				
Bond market	average government bond yield per year with rating AAA (in percent):				

The Thai questionnaire included the following markets: Thailand, China, Japan, USA/Canada, Europe, other Emerging Markets.

3) Task for surveys in Germany, Russia, Ukraine, and Thailand – presented in the version for Germany:

Apart from any fund's restriction – Please allocate an amount of 10 mn. € to invest in the following regions (adding up to 100%):

___ % Germany ___ % USA and Canada ___ % Emerging Markets

___ % Europe (ex. Germany) ___ % Asia

Home markets and regional groups were country-specifically adapted (as shown in Figure 5.2 in Chapter 5).

References

Adler, M., Dumas, B. (1984), Exposure to Currency Risk: Definition and Measurement, Financial Management 13, 41-50.

Aggarwal, R., Klapper, L., Wysocki, P.D. (2005), Portfolio Preferences of Foreign Institutional Investors, *Journal of Banking & Finance* 29, 2919-2946.

Ahearne, A.G., Griever, W.L., Warnock, F.E. (2004), Information Costs and Home Bias: An Analysis of U.S. Holdings of Foreign Equities, *Journal of International Economics* 62, 313-336.

Aitken, B. (1998), Have Institutional Investors Destabilized Emerging Markets?, *Contemporary Economic Policy* 16, 173-184.

Alpert, M., Raiffa, H. (1982), A Progress Report on the Training of Probability Assessors, in: Kahneman, D., Slovic, P., Tversky, A. (Eds.), *Judgment under Uncertainty: Heuristics and Biases*, Cambridge: Cambridge University Press, 294-305.

Arnswald, T. (2001), Investment Behaviour of German Equity Fund Managers: An Exploratory Analysis of Survey Data. Deutsche Bundesbank *Discussion Paper* 08/01, Frankfurt.

Arora, N., Ou-Yang, H. (2001), Explicit and Implicit Incentives in a Delegated Portfolio Management Problem: Theory and Evidence, *Working Paper*, University of North Carolina.

Avery, C., Zemsky, P. (1998), Multidimensional Uncertainty and Herd Behavior in Financial Markets, *American Economic Review* 88, 724-748.

Babilis, S., Fitzgerald, V. (2005), Risk Appetite, Home Bias and the Unstable Demand for Emerging Market Assets, *International Review of Applied Economics* 19, 459-476.

Banerjee, A. (1992), A Simple Model of Herd Behavior, *Quarterly Journal of Economics* 107, 797-818.

Barber, B.M., Odean, T. (2000), Trading Is Hazardous to Your Wealth: The Common Stock Investment Performance of Individual Investors, *Journal of Finance* 55, 773-806.

Barber, B.M., Odean, T. (2001), Boys Will Be Boys: Gender, Overconfidence, and Common Stock Investment, *Quarterly Journal of Economics* 116, 261-292.

Barberis, N., Shleifer, A., Vishny, R. (1998), A Model of Investor Sentiment, *Journal of Financial Economics* 49, 307-343.

Barberis, N., Thaler, R. (2003), A Survey of Behavioral Finance, in: Constantinides, G.M., Harris, M., Stulz, R. (Eds.), *Handbook of the Economics of Finance*, vol. 1B. Amsterdam: Elsevier, 1053-1123.

Barberis, N., Xiong, W. (2006), What drives the disposition effect? An analysis of a long-standing preference-based explanation, *SSRN-Working Paper* No. 12397.

Bartram, S.M., Brown, G.W., Minton, B.A. (2010), Resolving the Exposure Puzzle: The Many Facets of Exchange Rate Exposure, *Journal of Financial Economics* 95, 148-173.

Beckmann, D., Menkhoff, L., Suto, M. (2008), Does Culture Influence Asset Managers' Views and Behavior?, *Journal of Economic Behavior & Organization* 67, 624-643.

Beim, D.O., Calomiris, C.W. (2001), *Emerging Financial Markets*, New York: McGraw Hill/Irwin.

Biais, B., Hilton, D., Mazurier, K., Pouget, S. (2005), Judgmental Overconfidence, Self-Monitoring and Trading Performance in An Experimental Financial Market, *Review of Economic Studies* 72, 287-312.

Biais, B., Weber, M. (2007), Hindsight bias and investment performance, *IDEI Working Paper* No. 476.

Bikhchandani, S., Hirshleifer, D., Welch, I. (1992), A Theory of Fads, Fashion, Custom and Cultural Change as Informational Cascades, *Journal of Political Economy* 100, 992-1026.

Bikhchandani, S., Sharma, S. (2001), Herd Behavior in Financial Markets: A Review, *IMF Staff Papers* 47, 279-310.

Bodnar, G.M., Hayt, G.S., Marston, R.C. (1996), 1995 Wharton Survey of Derivatives Usage by US Non-Financial Firms, *Financial Management* 25, 113-133.

Bodnar, G., Dumas, B., Marston, R. (2002), Pass-Through and Exposure, *Journal of Finance* 57, 199-231.

Bodnar, G.B., Wong, M.H.F. (2003), Estimating Exchange Rate Exposures: Issues in Model Structure, *Financial Management* 32, 35-67.

Borensztein, E., Gelos, G. (2003), A Panic-Prone Pack? The Behavior of Emerging Market Mutual Funds, *IMF Staff Papers* 50, 43-63.

Cai, J., Chan, K.C., Yamada, T. (1997), The Performance of Japanese Mutual Funds, *Review of Financial Studies* 10, 237-273.

Calvo, G., Mendoza, E. (2000), Rational Herd Behavior and Globalization of Securities Markets, *Journal of International Economics* 51, 79-113.

Carhart, M.M. (1997), On Persistence in Mutual Fund Performance, *Journal of Finance* 52, 57-82.

Chamberlain, S., Howe, J.S., and Popper, H. (1997), The Exchange Rate Exposure of US and Japanese Banking Institutions, *Journal of Banking & Finance* 21, 871-889.

Chang, C. (2009), Information Footholds: Isolating Local Presence as a Factor in Analyst Performance and Trading, *Journal of International Money and Finance*, forthcoming.

Chari, V., Kehoe, P.J. (2003), Hot Money, *Journal of Political Economy* 111, 1262-1292.

Chevalier, J., Ellison, G. (1999a), Are Some Mutual Fund Managers Better than Others? Cross-Sectional Patterns in Behavior and Performance, *Journal of Finance* 54, 875-899.

Chevalier, J., Ellison, G. (1999b), Career Concerns of Mutual Fund Managers, *Quarterly Journal of Economics* 114, 389-432.

Choe, H., Kho, B.-C., Stulz, R.M. (1999), Do Foreign Investors Destabilize Stock Markets? The Korean Experience in 1997, *Journal of Financial Economics* 54, 227-264.

Choe, H., Kho, C.B., Stulz, R.M. (2001), Do Domestic Investors have More Valuable Information about Individual Stocks than Foreign Investors? *NBER Working Paper* No. 8073.

Choi, J.J., Prasad, A.M. (1995), Exchange Risk Sensitivity and its Determinants: A Firm and Industry Analysis of US Multinationals, *Financial Management* 24, 77-88.

Christoffersen, P., Slok T. (2000), Do Asset Prices in Transition Countries Contain Information about Future Economic Activity? *IMF Working Paper* WP/00/103.

Chue, T.K., Cook, D. (2008), Emerging Market Exchange Rate Exposure, *Journal of Banking & Finance* 32, 1349-1362.

Cigna, G.P., Chapaev, R. (2008), Securities Markets Legislation in Transition Countries: Law and Practice, in: *Law in transition 2008*, EBRD, 6-17.

Coval, J.D., Moskowitz, T.J. (1999), Home Bias at Home: Local Equity Preference in Domestic Portfolios, *Journal of Finance* 54, 2045-2073.

Coval, J.D., Shumway, T. (2005), Do Behavioral Biases Affect Prices?, *Journal of Finance* 60, 1-34.

Covrig, V., Melvin, M. (2002), Asymmetric Information and Price Discovery in the FX Market: Does Tokyo Know More about the Yen? *Journal of Empirical Finance* 9, 271-285.

Daniel, K., Hirshleifer, D., Subrahmanyam, A. (1998), Investor Psychology and Security Market Under- and Overreactions, *Journal of Finance* 53, 1839-1886.

De Bondt, W.F.M., Thaler, R. (1985), Does the Stock Market Overreact?, *Journal of Finance* 40, 793-805.

Deaves, R., Lüders, E., Schröder, M. (2005), The Dynamics of Overconfidence: Evidence from Stock Market Forecasters, Center for European Economic Research (ZEW), *ZEW Discussion Paper* No. 05-83.

Devenow, A., Welch, I. (1996), Rational Herding in Financial Economics, *European Economic Review* 40, 603-615.

Di Ioro, A., Faff, R. (2000), An Analysis of Asymmetry in Foreign Currency Exposure of the Australian Equities Markets, *Journal of Multinational Financial Management* 10, 133-159.

Diamond, D.W. (1985), Optimal Release of Information by Firms, *Journal of Finance* 40, 828-862.

Ding, B., Wermers, R. (2007), Mutual Fund Performance and Governance Structure: The Role of Portfolio Managers and Boards of Directors, *Working Paper*, University of Maryland.

Disyatat, P., Gelos, G. (2001), The Asset Allocation of Emerging Markets Mutual Funds, *IMF Working Paper* No. 01/111, Washington D.C.

Dominguez, K.M.E., Tesar, L.L. (2006), Exchange Rate Exposure, *Journal of International Economics* 68, 188-218.

Dvorák, T. (2005), Do Domestic Investors Have Information Advantage? Evidence from Indonesia, *Journal of Finance* 55, 817-839.

Edison, H.J., Warnock, F.E. (2004), U.S. Investors' Emerging Market Equity Portfolios: A Security-Level Analysis, *Review of Economics and Statistics* 86, 691-704.

Ehrlinger, J., Gilovich, T., Ross, L. (2005), Peering into the Bias Blind Spot: People's Assessments of Bias in Themselves and Others, *Personality and Social Psychology Bulletin* 31, 680-692.

Eichberger, J., Grant, S., King, S. P. (1999), On Relative Performance Contracts and Fund Manager's Incentives, *European Economic Review* 43, 135-61.

Eichengreen, B., Hausmann, R., Panizza, U. (2003), Currency Mismatches, Debt Intolerance and Original Sin: Why They are not the Same, Why it Matters, *NBER Working Paper* No. 10036.

Entorf, H., Möbert, J., Sonderhof, K. (2007), The Foreign Exchange Rate Exchange Rate Exposure Nations, Center for European Economic Research (ZEW), *ZEW Discussion Paper* 07-005.

Fama, E. (1970), Efficient Capital Markets: A Review of Theory and Empirical Work, *Journal of Finance* 25, 383-417.

Fama, E.F. (1998), Market Efficiency, Long-Term Returns, and Behavioral Finance, *Journal of Financial Economics* 49, 283-306.

Feng, L., Seasholes, M.S. (2005), Do Investor Sophistication and Trading Experience Eliminate Behavioral Biases in Financial Markets?, *Review of Finance* 9, 305-351.

Festinger, L. (1957), *A Theory of Cognitive Dissonance*, Stanford, CA: Stanford University Press.

Fischer, A., Isakova, G., Termechikov, U. (2009), Do FX Traders in Bishkek Have Similar Perceptions to Their London Colleagues?: Survey Evidence of Market Practitioners' Views, *Journal of Asian Economics* 20, 98-109.

Fischhoff, B. (1982a), For Those Condemned to Study the Past: Heuristics and Biases in Hindsight, in: Kahneman, D., Slovic, P., Tversky, A. (Eds.), *Judgment under Uncertainty: Heuristics and Biases*, Cambridge: Cambridge University Press, 335-351.

Fischhoff, B. (1982b), Debiasing, in: Kahneman, D., Slovic, P., Tversky, A. (Eds.), *Judgment under Uncertainty: Heuristics and Biases*, Cambridge: Cambridge University Press, 422-444.

Frazzini, A. (2006), The Disposition Effect and Underreaction to News, *Journal of Finance* 61, 2017-2046.

French, K.R., Poterba, J.M. (1991), Investor Diversification and International Equity Markets, *American Economic Review* 81, 222-226.

Friedman, M. (1953), The Case for Flexible Exchange Rates, in: *Essays in Positive Economics*, University of Chicago Press, 157-203.

Garvey, R., Murphy, A. (2004), Are Professional Traders Too Slow to Realize Their Losses?, *Financial Analysts Journal* 60, 35-43.

Gehrig, T. (1993), An Information Based Explanation of the Domestic Bias in International Equity Investment, *Scandinavian Journal of Economics* 95, 97-109.

Gehrig, T., Menkhoff, L. (2004), The Use of Flow Analysis in Foreign Exchange: Explanatory Evidence, *Journal of International Money and Finance* 23, 573-594.

Gehrig, T., Lütje, T., Menkhoff, L. (2009), Bonus Payments and Fund Managers' Behavior: Transatlantic Evidence. *CESifo Economic Studies* 55, 569-594.

Gelos, R.G., Wei, S.-J. (2005), Transparency and International Portfolio Holdings, *Journal of Finance* 60, 2987-3020.

Glaser, M., Langer, T., Weber, M. (2005), Overconfidence of Professionals and Lay Men: Individual Differences Within and Between Tasks?, *SSRN-Working Paper* No. 712583.

Glaser, M., Weber, M. (2007), Overconfidence and Trading Volume, *The GENEVA Risk and Insurance Review* 32, 1-36.

Glaum, M. (2000), Foreign Exchange Risk Management in German Non-Financial Corporations: An Empirical Analysis, in: Frenkel, M. Hommel, U. Rudolf, M. (Eds), *Risk Management: Challenge and Opportunity*, Springer, Berlin, 373-393.

Glosten, L. R., Jagannathan, R., Runkle, D. E. (1993), On the Relation between the Expected Value and the Volatility of the Nominal Excess Return on Stocks, *Journal of Finance* 48, 1779-1801.

Graham, J.R. (1999), Herding among Investment Newsletters: Theory and Evidence, *Journal of Finance* 54, 237-268.

Graham, J.R., Campbell, R.H., Huang, H. (2009), Investor Competence, Trading Frequency, and Home Bias, *Management Science* 55, 1094-1106.

Grinblatt, M., Titman, S., Wermers, R. (1995), Momentum Investment Strategies, Portfolio Performance, and Herding: A Study of Mutual Fund Behavior, *American Economic Review* 85, 1088-1105.

Grinblatt, M., Keloharju, M. (2001), What Makes Investors Trade?, *Journal of Finance* 56, 589-616.

Grishchenko, O., Litov, L., Mei, J. (2002), Private Information Trading and Corporate Governance in Emerging Markets, *Working Paper*, New York University.

Guo, W.-C., Shih, H.-T. (2008), The Co-movement of Stock Prices, Herd Behavior and High-tech Mania, *Applied Financial Economics* 18, 1343-1350.

Haigh, M.S., List, J.A. (2005), Do Professional Traders Exhibit Myopic Loss Aversion? An Experimental Analysis, *Journal of Finance* 60, 523-534.

He, J., Ng, L. and Wu, X. (1996), Foreign Exchange Rate Exposure, Risk and the Japanese Stock Market, *Working Paper*, University of Wisconsin.

Hens, T., Vlcek, M. (2006), Does Prospect Theory Explain the Disposition Effect? *Working Paper* No. 262, Institute for Empirical Research in Economics, University of Zurich.

Hilton, D. (2007), Overconfidence, Trading and Entrepreneurship: Cognitive and Cultural Processes in Risk-Taking, in: Topol, R., Walliser, B. (Eds.), *Cognitive Economics: New Trends*, Amsterdam: Elsevier, 225-235.

Hirshleifer, D. (2001), Investor Psychology and Asset Pricing, *Journal of Finance* 56, 1533-1597.

Hong, H., Stein, J.C. (1999), A Unified Theory of Underreaction, Momentum Trading, and Overreaction in Asset Markets, *Journal of Finance* 54, 2143-2184.

Hong, H., Kubrik, J.D., Solomon, A. (2000), Security Analysts' Career Concerns and Herding of Earnings Forecasts, *RAND Journal of Economics* 31, 121-144.

Huberman, G. (2001), Familiarity Breeds Investment, *Review of Financial Studies* 14, 659-680.

Ito, T., Lyons, R.K., Melvin, M. (1998), Is There Private Information in the FX Market? The Tokyo Experiment, *Journal of Finance* 80, 1111-1130.

Jegadeesh, N., Titman, S. (1993), Returns to Buying Winners and Selling Losers: Implications for Stock Market Efficiency, *Journal of Finance* 48, 65-91.

Jegadeesh, N., Titman, S. (2001), Profitability of Momentum Strategies: An Evaluation of Alternative Explanations, *Journal of Finance* 56, 699-720.

Johansson-Stenman, O., Martinsson, P. (2006), Honestly, Why are You Driving a BMW?, *Journal of Economic Behavior & Organization* 60, 129-146.

Jorion, P. (1990), The Exchange Rate Exposure of U.S. Multinationals, *Journal of Business* 63, 331-345.

Kahneman, D., Tversky, A. (1979), Prospect Theory: An Analysis of Decision Under Risk, *Econometrica* 47, 263-292.

Kaminsky, G., Lyons, R.K., Schmukler, S.L. (2001), Mutual Fund Investments in Emerging Markets: An Overview, *World Bank Economic Review* 15, 315-340.

Kaminsky, G., Lyons, R.K., Schmukler, S.L. (2004), Managers, Investors, and Crises: Mutual Fund Strategies in Emerging Markets, *Journal of International Economics* 64, 113-134.

Karlsson, A., Nordén, L. (2007), Home Sweet Home: Home Bias and International Diversification among Individual Investors, *Journal of Banking & Finance* 31, 317-333.

Keim, D.B. (1983), Size-Related Anomalies and Stock Return Seasonality: Further Empirical Evidence, *Journal of Financial Economics* 12, 13-32.

Keim, D.B., Madhavan, A. (1995), Anatomy of the Trading Process, Empirical Evidence on the Behavior of Institutional Traders, *Journal of Financial Economics* 37, 371-398.

Khoo, A. (1994), Estimation of Foreign Exchange Exposure: An Application to Mining Companies in Australia, *Journal of International Money and Finance* 13, 342-363.

Khorana, A. (1996), Top Management Turnover: An Empirical Investigation of Mutual Fund Managers, *Journal of Financial Economics* 40, 403-427.

Kilka, M., Weber, M. (2000), Home-Bias in International Stock Return Expectations, *Journal of Psychology and Financial Markets* 1, 176-192.

Kim, W., Wei, S.-J. (2002), Foreign Portfolio Investors before and during a Crisis, *Journal of International Economics* 56, 77-96.

Kiymaz, H. (2003), Estimation of Foreign Exchange Exposure: An Emerging Market Application, *Journal of Multinational Financial Management* 13, 71-84.

Kochetygova, J., Popivshchy, N., Shvyrkov, O., Todres, V., Liadskaya, C. (2005), Transparency & Disclosure by Russian State-Owned Enterprises, *Standard & Poor's Governance Services*, prepared for the Roundtable on Corporate Governance organized by the OECD in Moscow on June 3, 2005.

Konishi, M. (2007), A Global Network of Stock Markets and Home Bias Puzzle, *Applied Financial Economics Letters* 3, 197-199.

Koutmos, G., Martin, A.D. (2003), Asymmetric Exchange Rate Exposure: Theory and Evidence, *Journal of International Money and Finance* 22, 365-383.

Krause, A., Wie, K.C.J., Yang, Z. (2006), Behavioral Bias of Traders: Evidence for the Disposition and Reverse Disposition Effect, *EFM 2006: Symposium Behavioral Finance Discussion Paper* No. 63.

Kyle, A. (1985), Continuous Auctions and Insider Trading, *Econometrica* 53, 1315-1335.

Lakonishok, J., Shleifer, A., Vishny, R.W. (1992), The Impact of Institutional Trading on Stock Prices, *Journal of Financial Economics* 32, 23-43.

Langer, E.J. (1975), The Illusion of Control, *Journal of Personality and Social Psychology* 32, 311-328.

Langer, T., Weber, M. (2005), Myopic Prospect Theory vs. Myopic Loss Aversion: How General is the Phenomenon?, *Journal of Economic Behavior & Organization* 56, 25-38.

Levy, H., Sarnat, M. (1970), International Diversification of Investment Portfolios, *American Economic Review* 60, 668-675.

Lichtenstein, S., Fischhoff, B., Phillips, L.D. (1982), Calibration of Probabilities: The State of the Art to 1980, in: Kahneman, D., Slovic, P., Tversky, A. (Eds.), *Judgment under Uncertainty: Heuristics and Biases*, Cambridge: Cambridge University Press, 306-334.

Locke, P.R., Mann, S.C. (2005), Professional Trader Discipline and Trade Disposition, *Journal of Financial Economics* 76, 401-444.

Lütje, T., Menkhoff, L. (2007), What Drives Home Bias? Evidence from Fund Managers' Views, *International Journal of Finance & Economics* 12, 21-35.

Lütje, T. (2009), To Be Good or To Be Better: Asset Managers' Attitudes Towards Herding, *Applied Financial Economics* 19, 825-839.

Maug, E., Naik, N. (1996, last revised 2009), Herding and Delegated Portfolio Management, *IFA Working Paper* No. 223, London Business School.

Menkhoff, L. (1998), The Noise Trading Approach – Questionnaire Evidence from Foreign Exchange, *Journal of International Money and Finance* 17, 547-564.

Menkhoff, L., Schmidt, U. (2005), The Use of Trading Strategies by Fund Managers: Some First Survey Evidence, *Applied Economics* 37, 1719-1730.

Menkhoff, L., Schmidt, U., Brozynsky, T. (2006), The Impact of Experience on Risk Taking, Overconfidence, and Herding of Fund Managers: Complementary Survey Evidence, *European Economic Review* 50, 1753-1766.

Menkhoff, L., Nikiforow, M. (2009), Professionals' Endorsement of Behavioral Finance: Does it Impact their Perception of Markets and Themselves?, *Journal of Economic Behavior & Organization* 71, 318-329.

Montier, J. (2005), Seven Sins of Fund Management, *SSRN Working Paper* No. 881760.

Muller, A., Verschoor, W.F.C. (2006a), Foreign Exchange Risk Exposure: Survey and Suggestions, *Journal of Multinational Financial Management* 16, 385-410.

Muller, A., Verschoor, W.F.C. (2006b), European Foreign Exchange Risk Exposure, *European Financial Management* 12, 195-220.

Muller, A., Verschoor, W.F.C. (2007), Trade and Exposure of Eastern European Multinationals, *Emerging Markets Review* 8, 218-229.

Nickerson, R.S. (1998), Confirmation Bias: Ubiquitous Phenomenon in Many Guises, *Review of General Psychology* 2, 175-220.

Niessen, A., Ruenzi, S. (2009), Sex Matters: Gender Differences in the Mutual Fund Industry, *SSRN Working Paper* No. 1343490.

Nikiforow, M. (2010), Does training on behavioural finance influence fund managers' perception and behavior?, *Applied Financial Economics* 20, 515-528.

Oberlechner, T. (2001), Importance of Technical and Fundamental Analysis in the European Foreign Exchange Market, *International Journal of Finance and Economics* 6, 81-93.

Odean, T. (1998), Are Investors Reluctant to Realize Their Losses?, *Journal of Finance* 53, 1775-1798.

Odean, T. (1999), Do Investors Trade Too Much?, *American Economic Review* 89, 1279-1298.

Ong, L.L., Sy, A.N.R. (2004), The Role of Mature Market Mutual Funds in Emerging Markets: Myth or Mayhem?, *IMF Working Paper* No. 04/133, Washington D.C.

Otten, R., Bams, D. (2002), European Mutual Fund Performance, *European Financial Management* 8, 75-101.

Parsley, D. C., Popper, H. A. (2006), Exchange Rate Pegs and Foreign Exchange Exposure in East and South East Asia, *Journal of International Money and Finance* 25, 992-1009.

Preobragenskaya, G., McGee, R. (2003a), Corporate Governance in a Transition Economy: A Case Study of Russia, *SSRN-Working Paper* No. 459366.

Preobragenskaya, G., McGee, R. (2003b), The Role of International Accounting Standards in Foreign Direct Investment: A Case Study of Russia, *SSRN-Working Paper* No. 409020.

Preobragenskaya, G., McGee, R. (2004), Converting the Accounting System of a Transition Economy: A Case Study of Russia, *SSRN-Working Paper* No. 546343.

Pritamani, M. D., Shome, D. K., and Singal, V. (2004), Foreign Exchange Exposure of Exporting and Importing Firms, *Journal of Banking & Finance* 28, 1697-1710.

Pronin, E. (2007), Perception and Misperception of Bias in Human Judgement, *Trends in Cognitive Sciences* 11, 37-43.

Pronin, E., Lin. D.Y., Ross, L. (2002), The Bias Blind Spot: Perceptions of Bias in Self Versus Others, *Personality and Social Psychology Bulletin* 82, 369-381.

Pronin, E., Gilovich, T., Ross, L. (2004), Objectivity in the Eye of the Beholder: Divergent Perception of Bias in Self versus Others, *Psychological Review* 111, 781-799.

Reinganum, M.R. (1983), The Anomalous Stock Market Behavior of Small Firms in January: Empirical Tests for Tax-Loss Selling Effects, *Journal of Financial Economics* 12, 89-104.

Rozhnova, O. (2000), The Problem of Perception of the New Russian Accounting Standards, International Center for Accounting Reform (ICAR), *ICAR Newsletter* (December).

Scharfstein, D.S., Stein, J.C. (1990), Herd Behavior and Investment, *American Economic Review* 80, 465-479.

Scherbina, A., Jin, L. (2006), Inheriting Losers, *SSRN Working Paper* No 895765.

Schmidt, U., Zank, H. (2005), What is Loss Aversion, *Journal of Risk and Uncertainty* 30, 157-167.

Seasholes, M.S. (2004), Re-examining Information Asymmetries in Emerging Stock Markets, *Working Paper*, University of Berkeley.

Shapira, Z., Venezia, I. (2001), Patterns of Behavior of Professionally Managed and Independent Investors, *Journal of Banking & Finance* 25, 1573-1587.

Shapira, Z., Venezia, I. (2006), On Timing and Herding: Do Professional Investors Behave Differently than Amateurs?, *Working Paper*, The Hebrew University.

Shefrin, H., Statman, M. (1985), The Disposition to Sell Winners Too Early and Ride Losers Too Long: Theory and Evidence, *Journal of Finance* 40, 777-790.

Shiller, R. (1981), Do Stock Prices Move Too Much to Be Justified by Subsequent Changes in Dividends?, *American Economic Review* 71, 421-436.

Shiller, R.J. (2003), From Efficient Markets Theory to Behavioral Finance, *Journal of Economic Perspectives* 17, 83-104.

Shiller, R.J., Pound, J. (1989), Survey Evidence on Diffusion of Interest and Information Among Investors, *Journal of Economic Behavior & Organization* 12, 47-66.

Shleifer, A., Summers, L. (1990), The Noise Trader Approach to Finance, *Journal of Economic Perspectives* 4, 19-33.

Sias, R.W. (2004), Institutional Herding, *Review of Financial Studies* 17, 165-206.

Solnik, B. (2007), Are Financial Market Expectations Driven by Some Form of National Preference, *SSRN Working Paper* No. 1099914.

Stepanov, S., Pastoukhova, E., Gabdarakhmanov, S., Lazareva, O., Pankov, D., Sidorovskiy, E., Ukhaneva, O., Chernina, E., Shvyrkov, O. (2009), Transparency & Disclosure by Russian Companies 2009, *Joint study of Standard & Poor's and the Centre for Economic and Financial Research (CEFIR) at the New Economic School.*

Strong, N., Xu, X. (2003), Understanding the Equity Home Bias: Evidence from Survey Data, *Review of Economics and Statistics* 85, 307-312.

Stulz, R.M. (1981), On the Effects of Barriers to International Investment, *Journal of Finance* 36, 923-934.

Svenson, O. (1981), Are We All Less Risky and More Skilful than Our Fellow Drivers?, *Acta Psychologica* 47, 143-148.

Taylor, S.S., Brown, J.B. (1988), Illusion and Well-Being: A Social Psychology Perspective on Mental Health, *Psychological Bulletin* 103, 193-210.

Tesar, L.L., Werner, I.M. (1995), Home Bias and High Turnover, *Journal of International Money and Finance* 14, 467-492.

Thaler, R.H., Johnson, E.J. (1990), Gambling with the House Money and Trying to Break Even: The Effects of Prior Outcomes on Risky Choice, *Management Science* 36, 643-660.

Tversky, A., Kahneman, D. (1982), Judgment Under Uncertainty: Heuristics and Biases, in: Kahneman, D., Slovic, P., Tversky, A. (Eds.), *Judgment under*

Uncertainty: Heuristics and Biases, Cambridge: Cambridge University Press, 3-20.

Tversky, A., Kahneman, D. (1992), Advances in Prospect Theory: Cumulative Representation, *Journal of Risk and Uncertainty* 5, 297-323.

Visaltanachoti, N., Luo, H., Lu, L. (2007), Holding Periods, Illiquidity and Disposition Effect in the Chinese Stock Markets, *Applied Financial Economics* 17, 1265-1274.

Walter, A., Weber, F.M. (2006), Herding in the German Mutual Fund Industry, *European Financial Management* 12, 375-406.

Weber, E.U., Siebenmorgen, N., Weber, M. (2005), Communicating Asset Risk: How Name Recognition and the Format of Historic Volatility Information Affect Risk Perception and Investment Decisions, *Risk Analysis* 25, 597-609.

Weber, M., Camerer, C.F. (1998): The Disposition Effect in Securities Trading: An Experimental Analysis, *Journal of Economic Behavior & Organization*, 33, 167-184.

Wermers, R. (1999), Mutual Fund Herding and the Impact on Stock Prices, *Journal of Finance* 54, 581-622.

Williamson, R. (2001), Exchange Rate Exposure and Competition: Evidence from the Automotive Industry, *Journal of Financial Economics* 59, 441-475.

Wölfle, M. (2009), Information-Based Trade in Russia and the Effects of Listing Abroad, *Economic Change and Restructuring* 42, 229-262.

Studien zu Internationalen Wirtschaftsbeziehungen

Herausgegeben von Prof. Dr. Michael Frenkel

Band 1 Christiane Nickel: Insider und Outsider bei der Osterweiterung der Europäischen Währungsunion. 2002.

Band 2 Georg Stadtmann: Noise-Trader auf Devisenmärkten. Viel Lärm um Nichts? 2002.

Band 3 Wolf-Heimo Grieben: Trade and Technology as Competing Explanations for Rising Inequality. An Endogenous Growth Perspective. 2003.

Band 4 Alexander Mende: Order Flow Analyses and Foreign Exchange Dealing. 2005.

Band 5 Torsten Wezel: Determinants of Foreign Direct Investment in Emerging Markets. An Empirical Study of FDI Flows from Germany and its Banking Sector. 2005.

Band 6 Steffen Kern: The Behaviour of Interest Groups in Trade and Industry Towards Monetary Policy and Central Banks. Theory and Evidence on Germany and the Euro Area. 2006.

Band 7 Holger Michaelis: Kapitalbilanzliberalisierung in der Volksrepublik China und ihre Einbettung in den volkswirtschaftlichen Reformprozess. 2006.

Band 8 Ralf Fendel: Monetary Policy, Interest Rate Rules, and the Term Structure of Interest Rates. Theoretical Considerations and Empirical Implications. 2007.

Band 9 Katja Funke: Balance of Payments Issues in Central and Eastern European Countries' Run-Up to Euro Area Accession. 2007.

Band 10 Isabell Koske: Equilibrium Exchange Rate Models, the Euro and the 2004 Expansion of the EU. 2007.

Band 11 Dennis Stremmel: Protektionsmöglichkeiten in der WTO? Geistige Eigentumsrechte im TRIPs-Abkommen und die Forderung nach Sozial- und Umweltstandards. 2007.

Band 12 Daniela Beckmann: From Early Warning Systems to Asset Managers' Behavior: Evidence for Mature and Emerging Markets. 2008.

Band 13 Markus A. Schmidt: Information or Market Power: What is Governing Dealers' Pricing Behaviour in FX Markets? An Investigation in the Spirit of the Microstructure Approach to Exchange Rates. 2008.

Band 14 Jan-Christoph Rülke: Expectations in Financial Markets – A Survey Data Approach. 2009.

Band 15 Christoph Swonke: The New Open Economy Macroeconomics of Exchange Rate Pass-Through and Foreign Direct Investment. 2009.

Band 16 Dorothea Watzlaw: Der Weg der mittel- und osteuropäischen Länder in die Europäische Währungsunion. Aspekte der monetären Integration. 2010.

Band 17 Marina Nikiforow: Essays on International Asset Management: Evidence for Developed West and Emerging East. 2011.

www.peterlang.de

Kolibri 360 GmbH
Ferdinand-Jühlke-Straße 7
99095 Erfurt, Deutschland
produktsicherheit@kolibri360.de